MW01255157

Tabernacle of David

The higher worship of Mount Zion

By

Reverend Daniel G. Caram

Table of Contents

Foreword

To the average Bible scholar, the mention of "David's Tabernacle" usually draws a blank stare. How could anything this profound and obvious be so obscure? I believe that the Scripture is consistent in explaining this very point—that God purposely *conceals* truth in order to discover those who would seek the truth. Unto those who would seek and walk in the truth, God gives more truth. Understanding is a divine gift. As Jesus said: "No man can receive anything except it were given him from above" (Jn. 3:27). Therefore, as we undertake the study of this course, let it be realized that the author hopes only to impart *by grace* the same keys that holy men of God have passed on to him.

What is David's Tabernacle?

David's tabernacle was *a simple tent* that was erected upon Mount Zion. Unlike Moses' tabernacle or Solomon's temple, David's tabernacle has no description or dimensions given. It was simply an open tent. What makes this tent so special is the fact that it housed the Ark of the Covenant, which had no veil covering it. The account of this tent is given in the following passages: 2 Sam. 6:17, 1 Chr.16:1, 2 Chr.1:4. It is also alluded to in other places such as Psalm 15:1 and Psalm 24:3.

Why study David's Tabernacle?

As we are about to see, David's Tabernacle is a prefigurement of the Church. That in itself should demand our attention. If we do not understand the type, how can we understand the anti-type it represents? The Apostle Paul made this very plain in 1 Corinthians 15:46 when he said the natural must be understood before the spiritual. The study of David's tabernacle helps to give us a much clearer picture of the Church. All of these introductory truths will be examined again.

David's tent is analogous to the Church

The Scripture itself makes this analogy in Acts chapter fifteen, which is a record of the Jerusalem conference. All of the "well knowns" attended this convention, and one of the main items on the agenda was the Gentile infiltration into the Church. Even though Christ had commanded His disciples to teach all nations, the infant Church was still struggling to come to some unification on the issue of admitting the uncircumcised into their fellowship. After Peter's comments, Barnabas spoke, followed by Paul. Then James took the floor citing, Amos 9:11-12 as a defense. What James said in essence was that the Church is a revival of David's Tabernacle, and that the Gentile nations would seek its covering. (See Acts 15:15-17.)

These verses open a whole new panorama of thought, and in time will enable us to see the Church with a new vision. The author of Hebrews also informs the Church that our calling is not to Mount Sinai (which represents the Old Covenant, a covenant that Israel had no power to keep), but to Mount Zion. Mount Zion represents the promises of the New Covenant, because the Ark of the Covenant was there in David's tent (See Hebrews 12:18-24).

Let us therefore proceed to study this course with our hearts open to the truths of Zion's Tabernacle.

CHAPTER ONE

Understanding Types and Shadows

I n this first chapter of the book, I would like to devote a few pages to an aspect of Bible hermeneutics. *Hermeneutics* is "the science of interpretation." Most seminarians take this course as part of their regular curriculum. However, many lay people have not had this opportunity; therefore, an abbreviated section on principles of interpretation would be extremely helpful for this particular study.

The Scripture unlocks itself

The Bible interprets itself. There are keys within the Scriptures that help to unlock its pages.

Our defense department has always had a team of code breakers in order to unravel the messages of the enemy. However, in the realm of the Spirit, unredeemed man can never discover the code to unlock the divine mysteries. It is like Jesus said: *"Except a man be born again he cannot see the kingdom"* (John 3:3). The natural man receives not the things of the Spirit. Salvation opens our eyes for the first time. Consider the outer court fence around the tabernacle. That fence was five cubits high (about seven feet). Inside were all of the physical shadows and types of heavenly or spiritual truths. However, man had to first come through the gate of salvation before he could *begin* to see.

The Apostle Paul amplifies this point about types and shadows and their importance in Hebrews 8:5: "Who serve unto the example and shadow of heavenly things, as Moses was admonished of God when he was about to make the tabernacle: for, See, saith he, that thou make all things according to the pattern showed to thee in the mount."

Notice the phrase "heavenly things" and compare that with what Jesus said in John 3:12: "If I have told you earthly things, and ye believe not, how shall ye believe if I tell you of heavenly things." Actually, this is a very important truth when it comes to the laws of interpretation. We have to understand the natural truths before we can ever hope to see the spiritual truths. Below are a few simple illustrations:

Light and Darkness - (John 1:5) - "The light shines in the darkness, and the darkness did not overcome it" [NRSV]. In the natural, light is greater than darkness. As a matter of fact, the greater the darkness, the greater the light. This fact has a remarkable spiritual signification, for "greater is he that is in you, than he that is in the world."

Sowing and reaping - (Gen. 1:11) "And God said, Let the earth bring forth grass, the herb yielding seed, the fruit tree yielding fruit after his kind, *whose seed is in itself,* upon the earth: and it was so." In the natural every seed not only reproduces itself, but also reproduces *more.* Everything we do in life comes back to us. Words, gestures, thoughts, and actions are ways of sowing.

Reproducing like-kind - (Gen.1: 24) "And God said, Let the earth bring forth the living creature *after his kind,* cattle, and creeping thing, and beast of the earth *after his kind:* and it was so." Every living thing (whether animal, vegetable, or man) brings forth after its own kind. These are all natural laws, but they parallel spiritual laws.

Life out of death - When the Apostle Paul was explaining the resurrection to the Corinthians, he likens death to a seed being planted in the ground and decaying, and then out of that corruption springs new life (cf. Jn.12: 24). He further reinforces the fact that every seed reproduces *exactly* what it is, whether evil fruit or good fruit.

The heavens reveal resurrection truths - Paul then points to the heavens to show the distinction in the resurrection. Even as the stars vary in glory and beauty, and even as there is a distinction between the sun and moon, so shall it be in the resurrection—everyone has *a differing degree* of glory in the resurrection. (See 1 Cor.15: 40-42.)

Israel could not see past the physical realm

The teachings of Jesus were all rooted in the seeable, touchable, tangible realm. His parables, too, always related to the natural realm. They were teachings to which people could relate—the sower, the leaven hidden, the lost coin, etc. The problem with Israel was that they could not see beyond the natural. They could not see the spiritual implications. That is what the Apostle meant when he said, "the letter killeth" (11 Cor. 3:6). Israel interpreted everything at face value. That is why Jesus said to his disciples, "It is given unto you to understand the mysteries of the kingdom of heaven, but to them it is not given" (Mt.13: 11). The Lord purposely conceals truth so that He might discover those who are sincerely seeking truth. It is a point of grace!

"It is the glory of God to conceal a thing"
(Proverbs 25:2)

As the remainder of 25:2 tells us, "it is the honor of *kings* to search it out." The event of Christ's birth is a good example of this, for it was in fact *"royal blood"* that earnestly sought and found in a manger the hidden Christ and presented to Him their gifts of gold, frankincense, and myrrh. Do not miss this beautiful truth! The *royal* priesthood is one of the central themes of David's tabernacle. They had come to worship (Mt. 2:2). These seekers have a vision for the *throne.* There is something that is developed in our hearts by this quest that changes us into the image of the One whom we seek. It is only the worthy seekers who are made into kings and priests (Rev.1: 6, 5:10). In God's kingdom there are many levels of truth, and if we are not wholeheartedly pursuing Christ, many truths will be veiled from our eyes (Jn. 8:31-32).

Hosea 6:3 says—"Then shall we know, if we follow on to know the Lord." There are many things we will never come to know and understand if we do not "follow on" and "continue."

First the natural and then the spiritual
(1 Cor. 15:44-46)

There must be a grasp of the *natural* truths

before we can truly appreciate the *spiritual truths*. This is realized when we compare the differences between the Old Testament and the New Testament. The Old Testament is illustrated by natural types and symbols. The New Testament is the spiritual fulfillment of them. Let us contrast a few of these differences on the next page.

"First the natural, then the spiritual"

OLD TESTAMENT	NEW TESTAMENT
First Adam (old man)	Last Adam (new man)
Natural birth	Spiritual birth
Natural circumcision	Spiritual circumcision
Natural walk	Walk of faith
Physical journey	Spiritual journey
Physical weapons	Spiritual weapons
Physical children	Spiritual children
Physical inheritance	Spiritual inheritance
Earthly tabernacle	Heavenly tabernacle
Physical priesthood	Spiritual priesthood
Physical sacrifices	Spiritual sacrifices
Physical temple	Spiritual temple
Physical Jerusalem	Jerusalem above
Earthly Mt. Zion	Heavenly Mt. Zion
Law on stone	Law in heart
Letter of the law	Spirit of the law

Physical death   Spiritual death
                                 (second death)

The list goes on of "first the natural, and then the spiritual." It is so necessary to understand this principle. Many within Christendom discount the Old Testament and say it is not relevant, but *all* Scripture is given by inspiration of God and is profitable for doctrine, reproof, correction, and instruction in righteousness.

The New Testament verifies the Old Testament

The Old Testament contains all the truths of the New Testament, even though many of them were concealed. In the Book of Acts, the apostles did not have a New Testament from which to preach. The New Testament books were not collected and placed in the Canon of sacred Scripture until 396 AD. When Paul told Timothy: "All scripture is given by inspiration of God, and is profitable for doctrine, for reproof, for correction, for instruction in righteousness" he was referring to the Old Testament (11 Tim. 3:15-16).

What book did Jesus Himself point to? There was only *the Old Testament.* In fact, Jesus made this statement in John 5:39—"Search the scriptures; for in them ye think ye have eternal life:

and they are they which testify of me." After Christ was resurrected, He said to His disciples: "These are the words which I spake unto you, while I was yet with you, that all things must be fulfilled, which were written in the law of Moses, and in the prophets, and In the psalms, concerning me" (Lu. 24:44).

The Apostle Paul gives us some N.T. terminology to explain the O.T.

Galatians 4:24	"Allegory"
1 Corinthians 10:11	"Ensample" or (type)
1 Corinthians 10:6	"Example"
Hebrews 9:9	"Figure"
Hebrews 8:5	"Pattern"
Galatians 3:25	"Schoolmaster" (theories & principles)
Hebrews 8:5	"Shadow"
Hebrews 7:15	"Similitude" (likeness)

All of these terms tell us the same thing—that the Old Testament was just a prefigurement of that which was to come. The Old Testament is full of illustrations that bear New Testament significance— the Passover Lamb, the journey, the wilderness trials, and the Promised Land are examples. It is impossible to have any real authority in the New

Testament unless we can authenticate our doctrine within the Law, the Prophets, and the Psalms.

All the Biblical Laws of hermeneutics will agree

We have looked briefly at only one of these principles of interpretation—the law of "first the natural and then the spiritual," but even this is enough to set the stage for the truths of David's tabernacle. There are many truths that are difficult to understand; yet this one principle helps us to see things in a new dimension. Let us consider another passage. This one is in Matthew 11:12: " And from the days of John the Baptist until now the kingdom of heaven suffereth violence, and the violent take it by force." During the Old Testament age, the battles were of the physical nature. They fought against literal flesh and blood with a literal sword and shield. It was not so in the New Testament.

John the Baptist's short ministry began the transition from flesh to spirit. The battle is now moving into the heavenly sphere, and there must be a certain violence in the spirit to take the kingdom. John also challenged Israel on the grounds of their *physical circumcision* when he said, in effect, that God desired a *heart circumcision* to prove their connection to Abraham. (See Matt. 3:9-10.)

A personal experience

Before we proceed to chapter two, permit me to share a personal experience. Many years ago I was seeking for the truth and reality of the baptism in the Holy Spirit. I had heard all the arguments about the Pentecostal carnality and I didn't need to be convinced on that point since I had grown up in a Pentecostal environment. Yet I wanted to know for myself the truth and reality of this experience, if in fact it were real.

The outcome of my search was interesting. After an initial experience of being filled with the Spirit, I spoke in tongues. Still it was not the manifestation of tongues that convinced me as much as the spiritual illumination and the confirmation that followed. Like the man born blind in John 9:1, many are born into the kingdom with a veil over their eyes. Paul prayed for the Ephesians in Ephesians 1:18, that the eyes of their spiritual understanding would be opened. The baptism in the Spirit was very transforming. It awakened my heart and enhanced my spiritual vision considerably.

> *May I exhort those who have not known this experience to seek it! God does not give us a serpent [an evil spirit] when we ask for a fish. (See Luke 11:11-13.)*

CHAPTER TWO

Background of David's Tabernacle

I n this chapter, we are going to consider some of the historical backdrop of David's Tabernacle. We shall also consider some terminology and distinctions that will help us later in this study.

Mount Zion versus the City of Zion

Remembering that David's Tabernacle was resting upon Mount Zion, I think it would help us to understand the distinction between Mount Zion and Zion, the city. Mount Zion is a small physical hill within the city of Jerusalem, which is often called Zion. The psalmist said, "Glorious things are spoken of thee (Zion) O City of God." Here he is referring to the gates of Zion the city, or the city of Jerusalem (cf. Psa. 87:1-3). Jerusalem upon *earth* is always a figure of the Jerusalem *above.* Zion (the city) spiritually speaks of the Glorious Church. Mount Zion within the city speaks of a more exclusive place within the Church. We will examine this later.

*Note: Our high calling is to go up to Mount Zion, for this is the place of His habitation, the place of His throne. (See Rev.14:1-3.) Sin is to fall short of God's purposes. Therefore, if we do not move on in God, we are sinning. Sin is to come short of the glory of God (Rom. 3:23, Phil. 3:14).

Moses points the way

In Exodus chapter fifteen, Moses prophetically points to the mountain that God desired to bring Israel unto while they were still in the wilderness. Exodus 15:17— "Thou shalt bring them in, and plant them in the mountain of thine inheritance, in the place, O LORD, which thou hast made for thee to dwell in." In actuality, it would be another four hundred and fifty years before Israel would begin to see the reality of this. There was still much land yet to be possessed at the death of Joshua. Mount Zion in Jerusalem was still in the hands of the Jebusites, until David finally subdued it.

Moses called this mountain, "the mountain of his inheritance." Zion is often called "His dwelling place." As we shall see later, all of the greater promises of God are to be found upon this mountain. The interesting thing about this whole scenario is that it so typifies the plan of God. Let us use a verse to illustrate the point: Psalm 76:2 - "In Salem also is his tabernacle, and his dwelling place in Zion." Notice the distinction between Salem (a contraction of Jerusalem), and Zion. It is as though God withdraws Himself to His exclusive dwelling and looks for those who will seek Him there.

Let us consider another verse: Psalm 87:2 - "The LORD loveth the gates of Zion more than all the dwellings of Jacob." Here again the Lord shows his favoritism. God has His exclusive dwelling place wherein all the special promises, protection, and favor abide, and He seeks all those who desire to abide in this place. My purpose in relating all of this is not just to give us an understanding of the Kingdom levels, but to create a desire within us to ascend unto them. David had such a desire, and, of course, he is the one who sets the precedent in this study.

Moses' Tabernacle reveals three divisions

Moses' tabernacle will help us to further understand the background and the uniqueness of David's tent. Moses' tabernacle is a pattern of spiritual truths. It shows man the way to the fullness of God. "Thy way, O God, is in the sanctuary" (Psa. 77:13). This "way" starts at the *gate of salvation* at the opening of the outer court (eastward) and leads to the *glory* at the extreme end of the court (westward) behind the veil. Herein is the desire and the purpose of God—to bring "many sons unto glory" (Heb. 2:10). The entrance is wide. Whosoever will may come. And yet, the way becomes more exclusive (or more narrow) for those who desire to know Him in His fullness. This walk becomes far more restrictive as we go on, and yet there is far more reality as we do.

Moses and the Israelites are a good example of this. Moses was one who knew the Lord intimately, and thus, he was judged more severely than the other Israelites. Let us make no mistake about this! Moses was not allowed to "lose his cool" and blow up when he was provoked. There were many people who were far less worthy than Moses who entered the Promised Land. They were far less accountable than Moses. There is a big difference between laity and leadership. (See Heb.13:17.)

There are three main divisions in Moses' tabernacle, which reveal the three dispensations and also three groups within the Kingdom:

- **The Outer Court**—represents the age of the Law. From the Passover in Egypt to Christ our Passover was approximately 1500 years. There were 1500 sq. cubits in the outer court fence.
- **The Holy Place**—represents the Church Age. The measure of the holy place is 2000 cubic cubits. There are many types that indicate the age of the Church to be about 2000 years.
- **The Holy of Holies**—represents the Millennial Age. There are 1000 cubic cubits in the holiest place. There are 1000 years in the Millennial reign. The holiest place was where the Ark of the Covenant rested. The Ark symbolized the presence of God. Christ Himself will be present on earth during the Millennium.

The kingdom of God is always symbolized in the three levels:

- Outer Court   Little children
- Holy Place   Young men

- Holy of Holies   Fathers (See 1 John 2:13.)

Every section shows a greater dimension of the Word:

- Outer Court   (The Laver) Washing of water by the word (See Eph. 5:26.)
- Holy Place   (Table of Shewbread) Word becomes flesh (See John 6:55-57.)
- Holy of Holies   (Golden Pot of Manna) Hidden manna (See Rev. 2:17.)

The Holy of Holies speaks of the New Covenant, because the Ark of the Covenant was positioned there. When the Jewish nation rejected Christ, they refused the New Covenant and the possibility of coming within the veil during the Church Age. In the Millennium, they will receive Christ and His New Covenant. Christ was not only the messenger of the New Covenant, He was the very personification of it. He Himself is that Ark—the presence of God, God with us.

For us in the Church Age, the veil has been rent. We sit, as it were, in the middle section of the tabernacle scenario. We have access into the full realization of the holiest place, but the question still remains, will we enter in? "Seeing therefore it remaineth that some must enter therein" (Heb. 4:6).

Now that we have looked at the divisions of Moses' tabernacle, I think we will better understand the concept of David's veil-less tabernacle.

Historical account

During the days of Samuel, before David was born, we have the account of Moses' tabernacle while it was at Shiloh. Eli was the high priest, and the Scripture tells us that his sons (who were also priests) were wicked men. However, he allowed his sons to retain their priestly office (cf. 1 Sam. 2:12-36). It was because of this that God judged Shiloh and Eli's house. Chapters 4-7 give the record. Not only was this priestly family judged, the enemy also confiscated the Ark of the Covenant.

> *"He forsook the tabernacle of Shiloh, the tent which he placed among men; And delivered his strength into captivity, and his glory into the enemy's hand"*
>
> (Psa. 78:60-61).

* Note: Many of these Old Testament illustrations help us to understand certain concepts. For example, there are many who think that because the Church is God's house, it cannot fail. However, look at what happened to the sanctuary at Shiloh.

The Lord allows sin to exist for a time, but then He judges His own house and His own people! "For the time is come that judgment must begin at the house of God" (1 Pet. 4:17), (See also Jer. 7:3-14.)

Although Moses' tabernacle was a *figure* to teach people the way of approach to God, the very symbol of that which they sought [the Ark] was removed. 1 Samuel 4:22 records the incident like this—"The glory is departed from Israel: for the Ark of God is taken." Make no mistake about that piece of furniture. It was sanctified by the glory of God. That Ark could not even be viewed while it was in transit. It was covered, and when it came to rest it remained veiled (cf. Num. 4:5). Only the high priest was allowed to see the Ark, and that was only one day a year on the Day of Atonement. History tells us that the other priests would tie a cord to the foot of the high priest when he went beyond the veil. This was a precautionary measure just in case he was found unworthy in God's holy presence, was smitten, and could not come back.

There were often severe judgments associated with the Ark. Consider 1 Samuel 6:19-20: "And he smote the men of Bethshemesh, because they had looked into the Ark of the LORD, even he smote of the people fifty thousand and threescore and ten men: and the people lamented, because the LORD had smitten many of the people with a great slaughter. And the men of Bethshemesh said, Who is able to stand before this holy LORD God? and to whom shall he go up from us?"

The Ark helps us to appreciate the awesomeness of God. The presence of God is not something that can be tampered with or manipulated. There is no pat formula to bring God's presence, nor is there any way to subdue it when God moves. There is no way that you can box God into some canon or concept. God's presence can inhabit a carnal church that breaks all the rules (cf. Psa 68:18). "Thou hast ascended on high, thou hast led captivity captive: thou hast received gifts for men; *yea, for the rebellious also,* that the LORD God might dwell among them." Sometimes God gives extraordinary gifts to very unstable people just to keep them saved—"That He might dwell among them." God's presence can also be withheld for a season from a church or an individual that He is redeeming and refining. Job would be an good example of this.

> *Revival is like having the Ark in the Church. When the Ark is gone, the revival is gone, yet the people continue to go through the motions of worship; but it is not the same!*

The People yearn for the Lord

"And it came to pass, while the Ark abode in Kirjath-jearim, that the time was long; for it was twenty years: and all the house of Israel lamented after the LORD" (1 Sam. 7:2). The Ark had now been separated from Israel for about twenty years, and the people were just yearning for a fresh visitation. Often times God removes His presence from us to create a fresh thirst. (See Psa. 63:1.)

It is also interesting to note that during the days of Saul, the Ark was still sequestered in the woods of Ephratah, and Saul did not seek for it. Saul was not a seeker of God, and that seemed to characterize the spiritual attitude of the nation during his leadership. (See 1 Chr.13:3.)

*Note: In this study we will be reiterating certain important points from time to time. This is done intentionally to instill and impress certain truths upon our minds and hearts.

CHAPTER THREE

David Brings the Ark to Zion

I n this chapter we are going to follow David in his attempt and ultimate success in retrieving the Ark and bringing it to Zion. Bearing in mind that the Ark is symbolic of revival, we want to learn from the failure and rectitude of this endeavor.

In the conclusion of this chapter, David's Tabernacle will be planted upon Mount Zion, and this tabernacle will forever stand as an ensample to the Church Age.

(References: 2 Samuel 5; 6; 7; I Chronicles 13; 15; 16)

David, a pattern to the Church

The study of David's life is so important because David represents the true pattern for the Church as well as our individual lives: A division of his life is as follows:

- The Calling to Reign
- The Wilderness Experience
- The Three Anointings
- The Melchizedek Order
- The Authority over the Nations.

Saul represents Israel after the flesh. (The works of the Law)

David represents Israel after the Spirit (The Church Age). He opened the veil for Israel.

Solomon represents the reign of peace in Israel and the whole earth (The Millennium).

David's three anointings could be equated with the three divisions of Moses' tabernacle:

The Outer Court	David's first anointing	1 Sam. 16:13	(Called)
The Holy Place	David's second anointing	2 Sam. 2:4	(Chosen)

| **The Holy of Holies** | David's third anointing | 2 Sam. 5:1-3 | (Faithful) |

At his third anointing, David took Zion.

* Note: The three spheres of anointing on page 32 could easily have relevance to the Church Age. The *first* anointing is the baptism in the Spirit. The *second* anointing is the "Spirit of the Lord" anointing, which is the prophet's anointing (cf. Isa.11:2-3, Lu. 4:18). The *third* would be "the power of His resurrection," which is the Holy of Holies anointing. The Apostle Paul knew this mighty anointing (Phil. 3:11).

David's *first anointing* enabled him to slay Goliath and endure his wilderness preparation. David's *second anointing* enabled him to reign over Judah and to prevail over the remaining opposition. David's *third anointing* enabled him to reign over all of Israel and to take the last stronghold, the fortress of Zion. The last stronghold was the castle of the Jebusites.

The Jebusite stronghold

Spiritually, the Jebusites represent the discord sowers. One of the seven enemies that the Lord hates is the Jebusite: "When the LORD thy God shall bring thee into the land whither thou goest to possess it, and hath cast out many nations before thee, the

Hittites, and the Girgashites, and the Amorites, and the Canaanites, and the Perizzites, and the Hivites, and the *Jebusites, seven* nations greater and mightier than thou" (Deu. 7:1).

The seven nations mentioned in the above verse are analogous to the seven abominations which the Lord hates in Proverbs 6:16-19: "These six things doth the LORD hate: yea, seven are an abomination unto him: A proud look, a lying tongue, and hands that shed innocent blood, An heart that deviseth wicked imaginations, feet that be swift in running to mischief, A false witness that speaketh lies, *and he that soweth discord among brethren."*

The tongue is the hardest member of our body to control (Jas. 3:1-12). *Discord* is the last and hardest obstacle to overcome. True revival will never reside in a place filled with discord. Judas was the discord sower in the inner circle of which he was a part. (Compare Matthew 26:8-9 with John 12:4-5.) Judas was removed from the group *before* Christ gave his new commandment, His higher commandment of *agape* love. Agape means supreme love. Actually, you can never have unity as long as Judas is in the group, and you cannot "love" treacherous, false brethren.

* Note: Judas fulfilled the proverb, which describes *the dissembler.* Proverbs 26:25 says "there are seven abominations in his heart." Judas was

guilty on all seven counts! A dissembler is a man with two faces.

Anointing, likened to unity of brethren

"Then came all the tribes of Israel to David unto Hebron, and spake, saying, Behold, we are thy bone and thy flesh" (2 Sam. 5:1). It is interesting that the unity of the brethren is compared to the anointing of the high priest, and it is *only the high priest* that is allowed to enter the holiest place. "Behold, how good and how pleasant it is for brethren to dwell together in unity! It is like the precious ointment upon the head, that ran down upon the beard, even Aaron's beard: that went down to the skirts of his garments" (Psalm 133:1-2).

Although the stronghold looked impregnable, and although the Jebusites were saying, "thou shalt not come in hither, nevertheless David took the stronghold of Zion: the same is the city of David" (2 Sam. 5:7). It was almost as if the camaraderie of the brethren brought the anointing that destroyed the Jebusite's yoke.

Zion City now becomes the capital

As Psalm 87:2-3 says: "The LORD loveth the gates of Zion more than all the dwellings of Jacob.

Glorious things are spoken of thee, O city of God."
There is a reason God loves Zion more than all the
other habitations of Jacob. It is because David
brought the Ark of the Covenant to Mount Zion, and
Mount Zion became the symbol of God's dwelling
place. Psalm 68 is also a psalm of that era and it asks
this question in verse 16: "Why leap ye, ye high
hills? this is the hill which God desireth to dwell in;
yea, the LORD will dwell in it forever." Once David
took this city, he was determined to bring revival
into the midst of her. How different Saul's regime
was! They never sought after the Ark during the days
of Saul. This clearly shows the effect a leader has
upon the people and the nation as a whole.

Let us consider several verses that pertain to this
event: "And let us bring again the Ark of our God to
us: for we inquired not at it in the days of Saul. And
all the congregation said that they would do so:
for the thing was right in the eyes of all the people"
(1 Chr.13:3-4).

I think it is necessary to make a few comments
on the last verse. You will find all the background of
this verse in 2 Samuel 6 and I Chronicles 13. David
wanted revival and the people wanted revival.
Certainly there is nothing wrong with that. However,
because they tried to bring this revival about by
human effort and not in accord with the divine order,
the revival was blemished with a disaster!

Five cardinal mistakes

There are at least *five* obvious mistakes in their first attempt to have a revival. We will list them here and then give a brief comment on each one:

- There was no preparation made to house the Ark when it arrived.
- The musicians were unsanctified.
- The priests were unsanctified.
- They were not transporting the Ark according to the divine order.
- Man touched the Ark.

There was no preparation made to house the Ark when it arrived (1 Chron. 15:12-13). Several years ago there was a prophecy exhorting us to prepare the barns for the soon coming harvest. We need to prepare our house (naturally and spiritually) for His visitation.

The musicians were unsanctified (1 Chron.13:8 versus 15:12-24). Divine order was missing in their music. This revival had a lot of exuberance and human zeal. *Human emotion* does not bring the presence of the Lord, especially when the participants are not cleansed from the lusts of the flesh. Sanctification means to be separated. The blood only separates us as we *continue* to walk in the light (1 Jn. 1:7). Before real revival comes, the music ministry of the Church must separate from the world and the flesh. We will consider the music ministry later on in this study.

The priests were unsanctified (1 Chron.15:12-15). They had not appropriated the sacrifices necessary for their sanctification.

They were not transporting the Ark according to the divine order (1 Chron. 13:7, 15:2). They were not in accord with the Word. The priests were to bear "the Presence" upon their shoulders. Instead, they brought the Ark on an ox cart. These men were trying to bring in the presence of God in a fashion derived by their own minds. God would not tolerate it.

Man Touches the Ark (1 Chron.13:9-10,15:2). When flesh gets into the revival something will die. Actually the whole revival died (at least temporarily) along with the offender. God does not allow His types to be violated. When Moses was judged for smiting the rock twice, there was more to it than just smiting a piece of stone. The Rock was a type of Christ (1 Cor.10:4). Violating that type by striking the rock a second time distorts the Gospel message for all time. That action said Christ the Rock could be crucified a second time. Thus, we see the importance of types! "And David was afraid of the LORD that day, and said, How shall the Ark of the LORD come to me?" (2 Sam. 6:9).

The threshing floor

"And when they came unto the threshingfloor of Chidon, Uzza put forth his hand to hold the Ark; for the oxen stumbled. And the anger of the LORD was kindled against Uzza, and he smote him, because he put his hand to the Ark: and there he died before God" (1 Chr. 13:9-10). There are many insights to be gained from this first attempt to bring a revival, but I think the threshing floor sums it up quite vividly. The threshing floor is where the chaff is separated from the wheat. God often allows quite a shaking and a sifting to precede a new move. The offenders and the offences must go! That is a New Testament principle. (See Matt.13:41-43.)

Before the first *Great Awakening* took place in the eighteenth-century in New England, God dealt in unusual ways in the church where it all started. There were even untimely deaths, which brought the fear of God upon the Church. When Uzzah died on the threshing floor, David was smitten with a new sense of the fear of the Lord. (See 2 Sam. 6:6-7.) It is also conjectured that David penned Psalm 101 after the humbling of that incident. He said: "I will behave myself wisely in a perfect way. O when wilt thou come unto me? I will walk within my house with a perfect heart" (Psa. 101:2).

Revival begins in the home

Another valuable lesson gained from this tragic account is the place where the revival actually began: "So David would not remove the Ark of the LORD unto him into the city of David: but David carried it aside into the house of Obed-edom the Gittite" (2 Sam 6:10). Obed-edom was a Kohathite of the Levitical line. Here is where the revival began—in a man's house. The Church itself is only a collection of homes. If we do not have reality in our own home, then we can't have it in the Church. True repentance is evidenced by the attitudes of *being* (the "be" attitudes). This is why God is addressing the home today! (See Mal. 4:5-6.)

"And the Ark of the LORD continued in the house of Obed-edom the Gittite three months: and the LORD blessed Obed-edom, and his entire household" (2 Sam 6:11). Obed-edom's house was so blessed that all of Israel took notice. David, too, was stirred afresh for revival. Let us be encouraged by the "three months." When families begin to get things right in their homes, God can bring healing in just a short time. The outcome of this family is found in 1 Chronicles 26:4-8. All of Obed-edom's sons became mighty men of God.

* Please accept a word of caution concerning family seminars hosted by "the psychologist." There is no such thing as "Christian psychology." It only produces artificial fruit! Psychology is a diversion from the true anointing and attempts to *patch up* our fallen nature. The true anointing deals a deathblow to the fallen nature and brings true repentance and release.

The real revival comes

During this three-month interim while the Ark rested at the house of Obed-edom, a number of things got corrected:

- David prepared a place for the Ark of God (1 Chr.15:1).
- David appointed the Levitical musicians (1 Chr.15:16).
- The priests and the Levites sanctified themselves (1 Chr.15:14).
- Divine order was restored (1 Chr.15:12-15).
- David brings up the Ark (2 Sam 6:12).

"So David went and brought up the Ark of God from the house of Obed-edom into the city of David with gladness. And they brought in the Ark of the LORD, and set it in his place, in the midst of the tabernacle that David had pitched for it: and David offered burnt offerings and peace offerings before the LORD" (2 Sam. 6:12,17). The entrance of the Ark into Jerusalem was quite a jubilant occasion, and it must be noted that the music department was a key to the ushering in of the presence of God. Psalm 68 could well have been written upon this occasion: "Let God arise, let his enemies be scattered: let them also that hate him flee before him" (Psa. 68:1). The phrase, *"let God arise"* is always associated with the Ark in movement.

Psalm 24 might also have been penned in reference to this occasion. "Lift up your heads, O ye gates; and be ye lift up, ye everlasting doors; and the King of glory shall come in" (Psa. 24:7). History records that the gates of Jerusalem swung upward at that particular time. Gates speak of praise, according to Isaiah 60:18.

Michal despises David

"And as the Ark of the LORD came into the city of David, Michal Saul's daughter looked through a window, and saw King David leaping and dancing before the LORD; and she despised him in her heart" (2 Sam. 6:16). Michal is representative of the old order. Michal was Saul's offspring, and she never broke away from her father's house. (cf. 2 Sam. 6:20-21). One of the greatest hindrances to a new move of the Spirit is an attachment to the old regime. Many have camped around an old move of God, thinking that they have reached the zenith of spirituality. Michal *hated* the new move. She *despised* the physical manifestations as Israel rejoiced. She was determined to be loyal to her father and a past move of God. God pronounced barrenness upon her. She would ever be fruitless. Some of these thoughts will be considered and enlarged upon later.

The Tabernacle of David

Now we have finally arrived at the theme of this book: *"The Tabernacle of David."* The presence of God, symbolized in the Ark, is now resting in this unveiled tent. Suddenly we find the priesthood ministering in song and in sacrifice openly in His presence: "And he appointed certain of the Levites to minister before the Ark of the LORD, and to record, and to thank and praise the LORD God of Israel" (1 Chr.16:4).

One of the major differences between the Old Testament and the New Testament is the priesthood. We are *all* called to be priests in the New Testament, not as it was in the time of the Law when only the Aaronites of the tribe of Levi could be priests. David's Tabernacle stood for 45 years, and during that time there was *no veil* covering the Ark.

For this 45 year interim during the Age of the

Law, *anyone* who had "clean hands and a pure heart" could ascend this little hill and stand in God's presence before the Ark (Psa.15:1-5, Psa. 24:3-5). Normally, only one man, the high priest, could come in contact with the Ark, and that was only once a year on the Day of Atonement (Lev.16). David was directed by God to change the Mosaic order for a season during the Age of the Law. This was a very extraordinary 45-year epoch, for it permitted all men *who qualified* to approach the Ark in David's Tabernacle.

CHAPTER FOUR

The Significance of Zion's Holy Hill

I n this chapter we want to merge the thought of David's Tabernacle with the holy hill upon which it sits. What makes Mount Zion holy is the fact that the Lord has sanctified this hill by His presence. The Ark of His presence was there! For this purpose we want to magnify the significance of Mount Zion.

The Ark of the Covenant

Now that the Ark of the Covenant has been firmly established upon this hill of Zion, we understand why this hill becomes *the holy hill*. We are told in Leviticus 27:28 that anything that is devoted or given to the Lord becomes holy. This place was not only dedicated to the Lord, it was sanctified by His very glory! That is why the very name of Zion reverberates with awesomeness.

Consider again the Ark:

- It was symbolic of the New Covenant.
- It was symbolic of the Living Bread.
- It was symbolic of Resurrection Life.
- It was symbolic of the throne and the place of authority.
- It was symbolic of the glory of God.
- It was symbolic of Deity.
- It was symbolic of mercy and judgment.

Symbolic of the New Covenant (The law written within our heart)

After Moses first received the tables of stone they were broken. This signified that there was no power in the first covenant to keep it. Moses then went up the mount a second time and received another table of laws that were put into the Ark, signifying the law that would be kept (Exodus 19—34). The New Covenant was not attainable until Christ rent the veil. The Jews do not enter the New Covenant until the Millennium because they rejected

Christ, the only One who can help us fulfill the law (Heb. 8:7-13, 10:9-20).

Symbolic of the Living Bread

There was a golden pot of manna within the Ark. Jesus identified Himself as the manna that came down from heaven. (See John 6:31-32.) The promise to the overcomer is to partake of the" hidden manna," or hidden truths of God's Word (Rev. 2:17).

Symbolic of resurrection life

Also within the Ark there was Aaron's rod that budded. Jesus identified Himself as "the Resurrection and the Life" (See John 11:25.)

Symbolic of the throne and the place of authority

"The LORD reigneth; let the people tremble: he sitteth between the cherubims; let the earth be moved" (Psa 99:1). Between the cherubims that hovered over the Ark, Christ dwells. All power in heaven and earth belongs to Him. Christ was declared to be King at his birth, and at His death. His life on earth demonstrated what true authority is all about. Even the winds and the sea obeyed Him!

Symbolic of the glory of God

The glory of God covered the Ark (Lev.16:2). Christ was also glorified and the disciples saw His glory, especially on the Mount of Transfiguration. "And we beheld his glory, the glory as of the only begotten of the Father, full of grace and truth" (Jn.1:14).

Symbolic of Deity

The Ark was overlaid with gold and the gold, represents deity. His name shall be called Emanuel or "God with us."

Symbolic of mercy and judgment

Upon the Ark was the mercy seat. The highest aspect of God's nature is His mercy. Christ was the embodiment of mercy and righteous judgment (Jn. 8:16).

Christ—the fulfillment

Christ was the fulfillment of *all* that the Ark represented. When Israel crossed Jordan into the land of Promise, the Ark of God went first. However, there was a distance of 2000 cubits that separated them from the Ark (Josh. 3:4). This, too, had prophetic significance. Israel would not receive their spiritual inheritance until after the 2000 years of the Church Age. Israel as a nation would always have the "2000 gap" separating them from the Ark. This is because they rejected the Messenger of the New Covenant, which is Christ Himself. After the Church Age when Christ returns, Israel will receive their rejected King and enter into their spiritual inheritance. Dispensationally, Israel is still in the outer court.

David, for a brief period in Israel's history, housed the Ark in the tent he had pitched for it. That little tent upon the holy hill would become a figure of the Church in its highest dimension. James said that the Church is a revival of what David had on Mount Zion (Acts 15:16): "After this I will return, and will build again the tabernacle of David, which is fallen down; and I will build again the ruins thereof, and I will set it up." Mount Zion speaks of the fullness of what the New Covenant represents. To the Church, Mount Zion is equivalent to the holy of holies. For us the veil has been rent and there is access to it by His grace. However, it still remains to be seen who will fully apprehend the call.

Without a vision the Church dwells carelessly

Having a vision helps us to press toward the mark. It is like the parable that Jesus told of the hidden treasure (Matt.13:44). One man sees a treasure that others do not see. Therefore, he sells everything and he does everything in his power to gain that treasure. This is a kingdom principle.

When a minister says we have to coexist with sin in our life and that we cannot have the dominion over sin, he has just denied the New Covenant and the message of true grace. True grace enables us to have the victory over sin, yet we must press into God to obtain this grace. There is a price to pay to have our heart changed. Are you willing to receive grace? Grace is given *in time of need* (Heb. 4:16).

When a minister says that we have all the revelation we need and cautions people not to seek for the deeper truths, he has just denied the New Covenant. One of the promises to those who *overcome* is to "eat of the hidden manna." That, of course, is in the holy of holies (Rev. 2:17).

When a minister says that the day of miracles is over and that the Church can no longer demonstrate that power, he has just denied what the New Covenant provides.

A vision empowers one to press toward a mark, a goal. A president of a Bible school told me he had belonged to a denominational church that did not believe in healing. He was then asked to attend an ecumenical gathering of churches where they invited the ministers up to pray for the sick. Not only did he watch people receive healing, he himself was healed! He now preaches a fuller gospel.

"Ye are come to Mount Zion"

- Hebrews 12:22
"But ye are come unto Mount Sion..."

- Hebrews 12:23
"To the general assembly and church of the firstborn ..."

- Hebrews 12:24
"And to Jesus the mediator of the New Covenant ..."

In Hebrews 12:18, Paul had just told the Jewish Christians that their calling was not to Mount Sinai, but to the heavenly Zion. Mount Sinai represents the Old Covenant. Mount Zion represents the New Covenant. The whole overtone of the book of Hebrews is how much greater the New Covenant is than the old. The two covenants are then epitomized in the two mountains. There was a good reason for Paul's emphasis on the heavenly Zion. The Church in Jerusalem was actually digressing. They were reverting back to the Law, even to the point of offering animal sacrifices again. When people do not move on in God, they tend to go back into the old religion. Thus, the Apostle Paul redirects their focus to Mount Zion, the symbol of New Covenant reality.

Zion's mention

Zion is actually referred to in Scripture 153 times. This number is significant and shall be considered later in this study. However, I would like to make reference to a number of places where Zion is mentioned in Scripture, just to magnify its greatness. Again, bear in mind that it was the tent upon that hill that contained the Ark that made it *a hill of renown.*

- Psa. 2:6   Zion   place of ruling and reigning
- Psa. 128:5   Zion   where God commands blessing
- Psa. 9:11   Zion   place of His habitation
- Psa. 132:13-18   Zion   place of rest, provision, and joy

- Psa. 20:2   Zion   place of strength
- Psa. 133:3   Zion   place where God commands life
- Psa. 48:2   Zion   joy of the whole earth
- Isa. 2:3   Zion   symbolizes the higher standard
- Psa. 50:2   Zion   perfection of beauty
- Isa. 4:5   Zion   His glory is the defense thereof
- Psa. 69:35   Zion   symbol of salvation
- Isa. 14:32   Zion   the place of God's founding
- Psa. 78:68   Zion   place He loves (Psa. 87:2)
- Isa. 16:5   Zion   the place of God's judgments
- Psa. 84:7   Zion   meeting place with God
- Isa. 28:16   Zion   place of the "Measuring Stone"
- Psa. 99:2   Zion   symbol of God's greatness
- Isa. 31:4   Zion   the place God fights for
- Psa. 125:1   Zion   symbol of immovability
- Obad. 1:17,21   Zion   place of deliverance and holiness
- Rev.14:1-5   Zion   place of the throne and the choicest saints

These blessings listed on page 24 are just a few very good reasons to set our vision upon Zion's high call. David challenges us with the question, "Who shall ascend the hill of the Lord?" This makes it clear that there is a qualifying to do so. Not just anyone can ascend this hill and come into the holy of holies. It is only for those with clean hands and a pure heart. We shall consider the *qualifications* in a later chapter.

Note: Even after the Ark came down from Mount Zion to its permanent place in Solomon's newly constructed temple, Mount Zion still retained its distinction. This is because it would still represent the heavenly call.

Points to Remember:

- We must first understand earthly truths before we can understand heavenly truths.
- It is first the natural, then the spiritual.
- The hill of Zion was the most sacred place in all Israel.
- This is because the Ark of the covenant was placed here.
- God localized His presence on this little hill, in David's tent.
- This tent had no veil. Everyone who quali-

fied could come near.

- The Ark was accessible for about 45 years during Israel's history.
- David represented the Melchisedec priesthood of Christ.
- David was a priest / king who entered within the veil as a figure to all who qualified.
- He was a type of the coming Christ and the New Covenant and new priesthood.
- He prophesied of the new priesthood, and even acted out the new role (Psa.110:4).
- There are three levels on earth: the nation of Israel, Jerusalem the capital city, and Mount Zion in the city.
- There are three levels in heaven: the vast kingdom of heaven, New Jerusalem, and Mount Zion in the city.
- The earthly is a symbol of the heavenly.
- Revelation 14:1-5 shows us the summit of Mount Zion. It is the location of the throne.
- Mount Zion in heaven is the holiest place in heaven. This is where God dwells.
- The *choicest saints* are also upon this mountain "with the Lamb."
- Others are lower down the mountain. Some are in the city, New Jerusalem.

- Many others are outside the city and only know God from a distance.
- Let us ascend this hill of the Lord and seek to draw as near to God as possible.

Three Spiritual Levels

On Earth:

1.) The Land of Israel
2.) Jerusalem, the capital city of Israel See Psalm 76:1-2
3.) Mount Zion in the capital city of Jerusalem

In Heaven:

1.) The vast expanse of heaven
2.) New Jerusalem in heaven
3.) Mount Zion within New Jerusalem in heaven (Rev. 14:1-5)

The earthly is symbolic of the heavenly. Mount Zion (upon earth) is a figure of the most sacred place in heaven. This is the dwelling place of God. Though He fills heaven and earth, the Lord chose to put His presence upon Mount Zion as a figure of "the high calling." In heaven, this is the place of His throne. See Psalm 99.

*This whole figure serves as a pattern to those in the Church age. Spiritually, the high calling is to come up into the higher dimension in God. Let us not be content to dwell on the lower planes.

CHAPTER FIVE

The Melchizedek Order

*D*avid's tabernacle would be the presiding order until Solomon's temple was completed some 40 years later. One of the most outstanding features of this "order" is the fact that King David crossed the forbidden line of kings into the priestly function. Hundreds of years before the Age of the Law there was a King / Priest in (Jeru) Salem, and this man's name was Melchizedek (Gen.14:18-20). Melchizedek was a type of Christ and also a figure of the New Testament priesthood. This will be explained in this chapter. It was during this little interim of time that King David demonstrated the

"Melchizedek order." He set a precedent for the Church Age which we are just now beginning to realize and which must fully be realized before this Church Age ends! The Mount Zion order was instituted about 1000 years before the Church Age.

Melchizedek

The person of Melchizedek is often controversial. Indeed, there is a certain mystique and wonder about him. Some actually think that he himself was Christ. For this reason, we want to devote a few pages to consider just how great this man was and to see how he is a figure to our present dispensation. Melchizedek is only mentioned twice by name in the Old Testament, and yet the Apostle Paul spends three chapters expounding upon him and his significance to us (cf. Hebrews chapters 5—7). Let us now consider a few facts about Melchizedek:

- In the Old Testament, he is only mentioned in Genesis 14:18-20 and Psalm 110:4.
- He lived in approximately 2000 B. C.
- He was the king of Salem, or Jeru-Salem.
- He was the high priest of Jerusalem. (Remember, Zion was in Jerusalem.)
- He was without genealogy.
- He blessed Abraham.

- He served communion to Abraham (the bread and the wine.)
- He received tithes from Abraham.
- He is a type of the Lord Jesus Christ in Psalm 110:4.

Melchizedek - a type of the new priesthood of Christ

Paul, the theologian of the New Testament, makes several analogies of Melchizedek. He states that Christ is after Melchizedek's *order.* "Whither the forerunner is for us entered, even Jesus, made an high priest for ever after the order of Melchizedek" (Heb. 6:20). In essence, Paul is establishing the fact that Christ was both priest and king, as was Melchizedek. Under the Law of Moses, only an Aaronite from the tribe of Levi could be a priest, and only a descendant of David who was of the tribe of Judah could be a king. In Psalm 110:4, David prophesied of a coming new priesthood which would be after Melchizedek's order. Therefore, David was prophesying of a New Covenant that would replace the Old Covenant, for if the priesthood was changed, so would the whole Law have to be changed (Heb. 7:12).

Melchizedek was "the king of *Salem"* or Jeru-Salem (Heb. 7:1-2). Paul interprets "king of Salem" as *the king of peace.* "Salem" means peace. He then interprets the name Melchizedek to mean, "the King of righteousness." ("Zedek" means righteousness.)

Paul also mentions the fact that there was no recorded genealogy or record of this man's line. "Without father, without mother, without descent, having neither beginning of days, nor end of life" (Heb. 7:3). Genealogy was very important to the Jews, especially with respect to the priesthood or kingship, but Melchizedek had no genealogy. According to ancient history, kings in Melchizedek's time were *elected.* They did not inherit the throne by birthright.

There are many beautiful truths found in these chapters concerning the Melchizedek order of Christ, but to stay in the context and theme of this course, I want to focus on the King-priest who enters within the veil. As Paul points out to the Hebrews, the kingly line comes from Judah, and the priestly line comes from Levi (Heb. 7:11-14). These two lines could never cross; everything was reckoned strictly by genealogy. We have an account in 2 Chronicles 26:16-20 where King Uzziah tried to intrude into the priestly function, but he was smitten with leprosy. Thus, we see the seriousness of violating the genealogical code under the Old Covenant.

May I insert a little word of caution concerning

the need to "abide in our calling." We have seen people try to move presumptuously into an aspect of ministry that God had not chosen for them. The results were disastrous. For example, an evangelist is usually not a good teacher or a pastor, unless he has been given a double ministry. Paul exhorts: "Let every man abide in the same calling wherein he was called" (1 Cor. 7:20).

David crosses the forbidden line

In spite of the fact that the Old Testament did not make any provisions or exceptions to the rule, we now see David standing in front of the unveiled Ark and ministering before the Ark. In fact, as they were bringing the Ark up to the hill, David was clothed with an ephod. "And David danced before the LORD with all his might; and David was girded with a linen ephod" (2 Sam 6:14). *Only a priest* wore a linen ephod (Ex. 28:6).

David must have had quite a revelation of what had just transpired, because he writes prophetically of the coming Melchizedek priesthood in Psalm 110:4: "The LORD hath sworn, and will not repent, Thou art a priest for ever after the order of Melchizedek." What is so interesting about Psalm 110 is the fact that David was not only writing about the One who would fulfill this—he himself was experiencing what he was writing about. He was a king and a priest, and he had entered within the veil. None of this was according to the Mosaic Law, but David was moving under the anointing. Psalm 110 was written upon Mount Zion, and I term it "a Mount Zion Psalm."

The Royal Priesthood

God's original intention for Israel was for the whole nation be to a holy priesthood (See Ex.19:7). They were disqualified from that calling because of the incident of the golden calf (Ex. 32). It was at this time that the tribe of Levi stood on the Lord's side and was chosen for the priesthood. Levi proved their zeal for righteousness when they used the sword upon their own brethren who would not side with the Lord. (See Deut. 33:8-10.) A true minister does not *alter* God's standards because it is pricking his own house. We have known ministers who have upheld the truth until it offended their own house, and then they put down the sword of the Word.

Although Israel as a whole missed their calling to be a kingdom of priests and a holy nation, that same call has been extended to the spiritual Israel, the Church (Ex.19:5-6, 1 Pet. 2:9).

1 Peter 2:5

"Ye also, as [living] stones, are built up a spiritual house, *an holy priesthood, to offer up spiritual sacrifices,* acceptable to God by Jesus Christ."

1 Peter 2:9

"But ye are a chosen generation, *a royal priesthood, an holy nation,* a peculiar people; that ye should show forth the praises of him who hath called you out of darkness into his marvelous light:"

Revelation 1:6

"And hath made us *kings and priests* unto God and his Father; to him be glory and dominion for ever and ever. Amen."

Revelation 5:10

"And hast made us unto our God *kings and priests:* and we shall reign on the earth."

Hebrews 6:20

"Whither the forerunner is for us entered, even Jesus, made an high priest for ever after the order of Melchisedec."

The forerunner (Hebrews 6:20)

Observe the word, "forerunner." A forerunner is one who goes before us to show us the way. Christ not only shows us that we are called to be kings and priests, He has gone before and opened the way for us to enter within the veil. In a sense, all of the redeemed belong to the priesthood, and yet there are the three divisions that we could fit into:

- *A Levite* could function in the outer court.
- *A Priest* could function in the holy place.
- *The High Priest* could come into the holy of holies.

David's Tabernacle in a sense equates with the holy of holies. Christ has rent the veil and it is now possible to approach God, even to minister before His presence (See Heb.10:19-20). However, what so many Christians fail to see is that Christ not only paid the price to restore fellowship between God and man, He also was showing us the way to *regain* all of the reality and dominion we had lost by the fall. Indeed, the crown can be regained. If we miss this point, we have missed the whole theme of this study. David's Mount Zion experience bears this out clearly. When David took Zion he was given tremendous power and dominion over the nations!

The higher plane

Where was the tabernacle of Moses all during the time of David's Tabernacle? It was located at Gibeon! "So Solomon, and all the congregation with him, went to the high place that was at Gibeon; for there was the tabernacle of the congregation of God, which Moses the servant of the LORD had made in the wilderness. But the Ark of God had David brought up from Kirjathjearim to the place which David had prepared for it: for he had pitched a tent for it at Jerusalem" (2 Chron.1:3-4).

Consider this strange scenario: Gibeon was a little Levite town only six miles northwest of Jerusalem. At this time in history, the tabernacle of Moses and all of its sacrifices and ordinances were in operation here. However, the Ark of the covenant (which represented the object of their worship) was not in Gibeon, but rested in David's tabernacle on Zion's little hill in Jerusalem. Thus, there was *a divided worship* in Israel at that time. Technically speaking, we could say that there was outer court and holy place worship in Gibeon, but the holy of holies worship was on Zion's hill. Even though there was a very legitimate worship at Gibeon, the tent on Mount Zion was the one that radiated the presence and glory of God.

David had asked the question: "Who shall ascend the hill of the Lord; who shall stand in his holy place?" Very clearly, there was *and is* a higher plane of worship and spirituality for the people of God! Are you hungry and thirsty for something better today?

The veil

There are several ways one can view the veil. After all, the veil was the barrier between God and men. In one respect the veil represents the holiness of God. The veil had cherubims woven upon it, speaking of the holiness of God (Ex. 26:31). Or we could look at the veil from the perspective of Hebrews 10:20, which says that the veil represents our flesh. Either way, man cannot come to God because God is holy and man is a sinner. What would it take to rend this veil between God and man?

This is where the priesthood comes back into focus. A priest was to offer gifts and sacrifices for sin so that man could have restored fellowship. "For every high priest is ordained to offer gifts and sacrifices: wherefore it is of necessity that this man [referring to Christ] have somewhat also to offer" (Heb. 8:3). When a priest offered a sacrifice on behalf of the people, that animal vicariously took the sin and pain that the sinner deserved, thus providing a covering for the offender. However, the Old Testament sacrifices could never *purge* the stain of sin, only *cover* it (Heb.10:1-4).

Christ rends the veil for us, showing us the way

"Wherefore when he cometh into the world, he saith, Sacrifice and offering thou wouldest not, but a body hast thou prepared me" (Heb.10:5). This verse throws everything into an entirely different perspective. This great High Priest *became* the sacrifice. He vicariously assumes the sins of the world upon Himself and allows them to be nailed to the cross *by the offering of Himself.* "Jesus, when he had cried again with a loud voice, yielded up the ghost. And, behold, *the veil of the temple was rent in twain from the top to the bottom...*" (Mt. 27:50-51).

When the sin nature is crucified, the barrier is removed. Note carefully the following verses: "Having therefore, brethren, boldness to enter into the holiest by the blood of Jesus, By a new and living way, which he hath consecrated for us, through the veil, that is to say, his flesh..." (Heb.10:19-20). We can now come to God through the Crucified One, and only through Him!

What is our Forerunner telling us?

Christ is showing us the way into the fullness of blessing. However, this way into full blessing involves a total death to self. Christ's whole ministry demonstrated the *death to self* message: "Take up thy cross and follow me." Christ as a priest had to offer up a sacrifice, and it was His own body. What do you think we as priests are to offer up? Paul made this quite plain in Romans 12:1: "I beseech you therefore, brethren, by the mercies of God, that ye present *your bodies* a living sacrifice, holy, acceptable unto God, which is your reasonable service."

We must die *daily* to the old nature, and in doing so, we can come into that experience of being crucified with Christ. Paul said: "I am crucified with Christ: nevertheless I live; yet not I, but Christ liveth in me: and the life which I now live in the flesh I live by the faith of the Son of God" (Gal. 2:20). The reason Paul's life demonstrated the "reigning" aspect of Christ was because Paul first knew the priestly aspect. Even the demons moved aside for Paul (Acts 19:15). Paul knew the power of Christ's resurrection because he effectively experienced His crucifixion.

One of the misconceptions in the Church world today concerns the issue of authority. There is much emphasis on authority and taking dominion. There is nothing wrong with this in itself. The problem resides in "the ways and means" of taking that authority. Ruling and reigning begins by ruling our own life first, as it says in Proverbs 16:32: "He that ruleth his spirit is greater than he that taketh a city." When Christians have never learned to be *under* authority, they cannot be entrusted to exercise authority. Christ Himself was under authority. Our whole military system functions through various levels of authority. The real power belongs to those who have been disciplined to obey!

Christ reigns through His crucified ones

God does not lightly entrust His authority to people who have not died to self or who have self still on the throne. People who have the real power use it with great discipline. The Melchizedek order is twofold—the ministries of priest and king. The priestly order must precede the kingly order. We must suffer before we reign. David's ascent to Mount Zion was a very costly one. David suffered very much before he experienced his enemies becoming his footstool. In fact, many of Christ's sufferings are seen in David's psalms. We will consider the kingly aspect in another chapter.

Spiritual sacrifices we can make

In concluding this chapter, I would like to list a few of the spiritual offerings and sacrifices that we can offer to God through Christ. Peter said: "Ye also, as lively stones, are built up a spiritual house, an holy priesthood, to offer up spiritual sacrifices, acceptable to God by Jesus Christ" (1 Pet. 2:5).

Sacrifice of prayer	(Psa. 141:2)
Sacrifice of lifting hands	(Psa. 141:2)
Sacrifice of giving	(Heb. 13:16)
Sacrifice of praise	(Heb. 13:15)
Sacrifice of thanksgiving	(Psa. 69:30-31)
Sacrifice and service of faith	(Phil. 2:17)
Sacrifice of joy	(Psa. 27:6)
Sacrifice of righteousness	(Psa. 4:5)
Sacrifice of a broken spirit	(Psa. 51:17)
Sacrifice of total consecration	(Rom. 12:1)

There are many other sacrifices alluded to, and perhaps fulfilled in the two great commandments. (Mark 12:28-33). The thought of sacrifice tells us that there is a price to pay. Sometimes it is very costly to give thanks and have joy in the midst of a tragic situation. We often recall the verses that tell us that God's house is a house of prayer, but it is also called a house of sacrifice (2 Chr. 7:12).

Christ fulfilled all the offerings in His "once for all" offering at the cross. There were five major offerings He fulfilled, and they are mentioned in Leviticus chapters 1-7. Christ fulfilled them in the sequence given in Leviticus—beginning at the burnt offering—"I come to do thy will", and ending at the trespass offering for sin. Of course, His offering was not for His sins, but for ours. "Yet it pleased the LORD to bruise him; he hath put him to grief: when thou shalt make his soul an offering for sin" (Isa 53:10). As Christians, we fulfill these offerings in the reverse order. We begin our experience at the cross where we appropriate the trespass offering. We end our experience at the burnt offering which Paul tells us "is our reasonable service."

Power to bless

In Leviticus 9:22-24, *all* of the required offerings were offered. Moses and Aaron then went into the tabernacle, and coming out again pronounced the blessing. After this, the glory of God fell upon the people! "And Moses and Aaron went into the tabernacle of the congregation, and came out, and blessed the people: and the glory of the LORD appeared unto all the people."

Do you see the divine procedure? As priests we must also fulfill the necessary offerings which allow us to come into His presence, that we might come out with power to bless, and power over our enemies. David fulfilled many of the spiritual sacrifices listed on page 72. These fulfillments are found throughout the Psalms.

A healthy balance

During the Charismatic renewal, many of God's people came into new freedom. They came into the revelation of this New Testament king / priesthood. Many Catholics, for example, came to the realization that they no longer needed the Roman Church to intercede for them, but that they, as priests, could come to God through Christ.

Others in this movement were captivated with the ruling aspect of this order, trying to "take authority" over everything. Still others drifted into a prosperity emphasis which produced a self-seeking gospel. Thus, we can see the need for perfect balance in every area of truth.

The Church needs a healthy and balanced understanding of the Melchizedek priesthood. Often the true priestly ministry involves suffering and discipline. Because of this, some Christians go to the other extreme and put their emphasis on *death to self* with no emphasis on the resurrection power. God desires His people to know both aspects of this priesthood—the suffering and the glory. The new Melchizedek priesthood order means that we are being made into both priests and kings.

The priestly aspect involves suffering and sacrifice. The kingly aspect involves authority and rulership. Zechariah had a glimpse of the new *priest / king* order. He prophesied of Christ, saying: "Even he shall build the temple of the LORD; and he shall bear the glory, and shall sit and rule upon his throne; and he shall be a priest upon his throne" (Zec. 6:13).

CHAPTER SIX

To Rule and Reign

David's Tabernacle represents the position of those who have overcome and are reigning. Christ will have a group that emerges from His Church who have learned to reign in this life. Those who reign in this life will also reign in the Millennium and in the ages to come. In this chapter, we are going to see the *kingly* aspect of this Melchizedek order to which we are called. Continue to bear in mind that David (in figure) has set a precedent for the Church to which we have not yet fully measured.

A Mount Zion psalm of David

Psalm 110

"The LORD said unto my Lord, Sit thou at my

right hand, until I make thine enemies thy footstool. The LORD shall send the rod of thy strength out of Zion: rule thou in the midst of thine enemies. The LORD hath sworn, and will not repent, Thou art a priest for ever after the order of Melchizedek" (Psa 110:1-2,4). Although these passages are prophetic of the Second Coming of Christ, David himself fulfilled them. David's experience upon Mount Zion fore-shadows the true Church order. David, in his Mount Zion position, was given dominion over many nations.

"Sit Thou"

God desires His people to come into this *secret place of His dwelling,* this place of empowering. God has purposed that His people should rule in the midst of their enemies. In David, God shows us His desire for the Church. Observe the word "sit" in verse one. David would actually come in and sit before the Lord before the unveiled Ark: "Then went King David in, and sat before the LORD, and he said, Who am I, O Lord GOD? and what is my house, that thou hast brought me hitherto?" (2 Sam. 7:18). *Sitting* has the sense of having dominion! Notice what is said of Christ after His defeat of Satan at the cross: "But this man, after he had offered one sacrifice for sins for ever, *sat down*

on the right hand of God; From henceforth
expecting till his enemies be made his footstool"
(Heb.10:12-13).

The priestly order must precede the reigning or
kingly order. As we identify with the *priestly*
ministry of Christ, then we can know Him in the
reigning dimension. Paul confirms this clearly,
saying: "If we suffer, we shall also reign with him"
(2 Tim 2:12).

Christ sits at the right hand of the Father, expecting His enemies to be brought under His feet. How
is this to happen? — Through the Church, His body!
David said: "I have pursued mine enemies, and over-
taken them: neither did I turn again till they were
consumed. I have wounded them that they were not
able to rise: they are fallen under my feet" (Psa.
18:37-38). The Apostle Paul adds: "The God of
peace shall bruise Satan under *your* feet shortly"
(Rom 16:20). It is the destiny of the Church to
triumph over Satan. This goes back to the promise in
Eden (Gen. 3:15).

A minister once related a story about a country
that was crying out to God for a spiritual breakthrough. One day several of the angelic princes that
ruled that nation appeared before the minister. They
knew they had been defeated and just bowed before
the man of God, and he put his foot upon their
necks!

David rules and reigns

We must always think of David as a figure of the Church, because he personifies the Church that has entered within the veil. We could also think of the tabernacle of David as the fullness of Christ. Christ physically came from David. For about ten years David triumphed mightily as he maintained his abiding place on the holy hill. (This was before his terrible fall into adultery.) But for this short interim of time, David ruled the nations with a rod of iron—the evil nations! David wrote psalms 9 and 10 as he triumphed over the wicked nations. He stated: "The wicked shall be turned into hell, and all the nations that forget God" (Psa. 9:17).

Let us consider another "Mount Zion Psalm" of David—Psalm 2: "Yet have I set my king upon my holy hill of Zion. Ask of me, and I shall give thee the heathen for thine inheritance, and the uttermost parts of the earth for thy possession. Thou shalt break them with a rod of iron; thou shalt dash them in pieces like a potter's vessel" (Psa. 2:6, 8-9). The New Testament counterpart of this is seen in Revelation 12:5.

Until this time in Israel's history, their battles basically had been *internal*. Their enemies were within their territory or they fought against invaders into their territory. Their battles were not in the conquest of other kingdoms. However, after David's tabernacle was planted upon Zion, David was given the dominion over all the surrounding nations:

To the north	Zobah and Syria	As far north as the Euphrates (2 Sam. 8:3-6)
To the east	Moab and Ammon	(2 Sam. 8:2, 10:1-19)
To the south	Edom	(2 Sam. 8:14)
To the west	Philistia	(2 Sam. 8:1)

David not only subdues the surrounding nations, but he subjugates them. They were made to serve Israel and were put under tribute. Here is a true example of God's people becoming the head and becoming renowned among the nations.

Some of David's conquests

(2 Samuel 8:2)
"And so the Moabites became David's servants, and brought gifts."

(2 Samuel 8:6)
"Then David put garrisons in Syria of Damascus: and the Syrians became servants to David, and brought gifts. And the LORD preserved David whithersoever he went."

(2 Samuel 8:7)
"And David took the shields of gold that were on the servants of Hadadezer, and brought them to Jerusalem."

(2 Samuel 8:8)
"King David took exceeding much brass."

(2 Samuel 8:10-11)
"And Joram brought with him vessels of silver, and vessels of gold, and vessels of brass: Which also king David did dedicate unto the LORD, with the silver and gold that he had dedicated of all nations which he subdued;"

(2 Samuel 8:13)
"And David gat him a name when he returned from smiting of the Syrians in the valley of salt, being eighteen thousand men."

(2 Samuel 8:14)
"And he put garrisons in Edom; throughout all Edom put he garrisons, and all they of Edom became David's servants. And the LORD preserved David whithersoever he went."

(2 Samuel 7:1)
"And it came to pass, when the king sat in his house, and the LORD had given him rest round about from all his enemies..."

The enemies are symbolic

I think we could better appreciate some of these truths if we could bring them into a New Testament perspective. Obviously, we are not warring against physical armies or physical kingdoms in this dispensation. Instead, we are called to a very real battle in the realm of the Spirit: "For we wrestle not against flesh and blood, but against principalities, against powers, against the rulers of the darkness of this world, against spiritual wickedness in high places" (Eph. 6:12, cf. 1 Tim. 6:12).

In actuality, the Church still battles against the same ancient foes that Israel fought. We should realize that these enemies of Israel are still here spiritually. Those ancient foes all represent various works of the flesh. However, some of Israel's enemies are still quite literal. For example, the Palestinians are the Philistines.

Philistia — speaks of envy, hatred, and jealousy
Moab — speaks of pride and anger

Edom — speaks of bitterness, resentfulness
Babylon — speaks of confusion
Egypt — speaks of worldliness
Assyria — speaks of stoutness of heart and cruelty
Amalek — speaks of the lusts of the flesh

The enemy list is quite lengthy. These enemies reside both in the realm of our old Adamic nature and in the realm of the spirit (Gal. 5:19-21). These enemies are intangible and spiritual; therefore, they can only be dislodged by the use of spiritual weapons. I have singled out *three* enemies particularly because David mentions them in Psalm 108:9-10: *"Moab* is my washpot; over *Edom* will I cast out my shoe; over *Philistia* will I triumph. Who will bring me into the strong city? who will lead me into Edom?"

David was given the dominion over all his enemies. Let us first consider a grievous enemy, Edom. The Edomites were Esau's offspring. These represent people who have sold their birthright and are poisoned with bitterness and hatred against those who still retain their birthright (Heb. 12:15-16). Their grudge is perpetual against the righteous (Eze. 35:5). Esau was the offended brother who never forgave Jacob.

Edom looked like an impossible fortress. The capital of Edom was Petra, a massive fortress of rock. This seemingly impenetrable fortress of the

Edomites is like "the offended brother" of Proverbs 18:19: "A brother offended is harder to be won than a strong city: and their contentions are like the bars of a castle." There are people like this in the Church. However, Psalm 108 ends on a note of triumph. "Through God we shall do valiantly: for he it is that shall tread down our enemies" (Psa.108:13). David was victorious over the Edomites. Let us not be overcome with evil, but overcome evil with good (Rom.12:21).

*The phrase, "over *Edom* will I cast out my shoe" is just metaphoric for the diminishing of Edom. Edom would become like a refuse heap.

Victory in the Greater Son of David

God wants to give us complete victory over the fallen nature and the spiritual strongholds as well! The Philistines speak of envy (cf. Gen. 26:12-15). These seek to stop up our wells. Saul could not conquer the Philistines because Saul himself was possessed with envy. Envy and jealousy exist because the motives are not right. If our motive is to glorify God and not ourselves, we will never be troubled with jealousy. David's motives were pure and he was able to conquer the Philistines.

Saul would not destroy the Amalekites when he was empowered and commissioned to do so.

Therefore, the Amalekites ended up destroying him (2 Sam. 1:13-14)! Amalek represents the lusts of the flesh. The Amalekites were the offspring of Esau, the line of the flesh (Gen. 36:8-12).

Moab speaks of *pride* which produces wrath (Jer. 48:29-30). King David allowed God to do a deep work of humility in his heart, and because of this, he was able to defeat Moab (pride). There is a price to pay to have our heart changed. All of the fruits of the Spirit can be ours if we allow God to do His work in our lives.

Can you see this? From the Mount Zion position, none of these enemies could prevail against David. These are the same enemies that violently opposed Christ—envy, and pride, and hatred . See Matthew 27:17-18, Mark 15:10, Luke 11:53-54. They could not prevail against Him in life, and in death, He triumphed over them at the cross!

One of the questions Jesus asked the Pharisees concerned the lineage of the Christ. He asked: "If Christ is the son of David, why does David call him Lord?" (See Mt. 22:42-45.) They were unable to answer the question! Although Christ created David, yet Christ would later descend through David. In the purposes of God, Christ allowed Himself, as the eternal Son of God, to be made an embryo in the womb of Mary, who herself was David's offspring. The incarnation took place 1000 years after David.

Had David's throne been in existence in Jerusalem at the time of Christ, His genealogy would have made him King. See Matthew 1:1-16 and Luke 3:22-38 for His genealogies.

Jesus Christ was and is LORD

Christ did not ride on a white horse or sit on a throne. He did not wear a physical crown or any regal apparel, yet He demonstrated all of the kingly aspects of ruling and reigning. He ruled in the midst of His enemies with wisdom, mercy, judgment, and authority. Jesus Christ was in total command of every situation: "Lord" means *absolute ruler.*

Christ has all authority

- *Authority over the spirit world* (Luke 4:36): "What a word is this! for with authority and power he commandeth the unclean spirits, and they come out."
- *Authority over natural elements* (Matthew 8:27) "But the men marvelled, saying, What manner of man is this, that even the winds and the sea obey him!"
- *Authority over all sickness and disease* (Luke 7:22) "The blind see, the lame walk, the lepers are cleansed, the deaf hear, the

dead are raised, to the poor the gospel is preached."

- *Authority over all human limitation* (Luke 4:29-30) "But he passing through the midst of them went his way." He passed through the mob in the intangible dimension, knowing it was not His time.

- *Authority over hunger and the economy* (Matthew 15:33) "And his disciples say unto him, Whence should we have so much bread in the wilderness, as to fill so great a multitude?" He commanded bread and fed over 5000 men.

- *Authority over His House* (Mark 11:15-17) "And they come to Jerusalem: and Jesus went into the temple, and began to cast out them that sold and bought in the temple... And he taught, saying unto them, Is it not written, My house shall be called of all nations the house of prayer."

- *Authority over Satan and the sin nature* (John 14:30) "For the prince of this world cometh, and hath nothing in me."

- *Authority over life and deat*h (John 10:18) "No man taketh it from me, but I lay it down of myself. I have power to lay it down, and I have power to take it again.

This commandment have I received of my
Father."

Those who receive an abundance of grace shall reign in life

This Greater Son of David demonstrated the
Melchizedek order to which we are called: "...And
hast made us unto our God kings and priests: and we
shall reign on the earth" (Rev. 5:10). We might say,
"That's for the next dispensation," but not according
to St. Paul, who stated: "They which receive abun-
dance of grace and the gift of righteousness shall
reign in life by one, Jesus Christ" (Rom. 5:17).

Paul knew victorious reigning in every circum-
stance. Whether he was in a prison or in a palace, Paul
found the grace to rejoice and to be thankful. When
you can praise God at midnight after being beaten and
thrust into the lowest prison, you are reigning! (See
Acts 16:23-2.) Paul ruled in the midst of the storm!
Paul took authority over spiritual powers, over
diseases, and over the serpent's bite. Paul preached,
demonstrated. and lived the Melchizedek order in his
own life. This is the order to which we are called.

We need to have a clear picture of what true
reigning is all about. The Corinthians *thought* they
were reigning (1 Cor. 4:8). The Laodiceans also
thought they were reigning, but God saw them very

differently. He said they were "wretched, miserable, poor, blind, and naked" (Rev. 3:17). Then He urged them to pay the price: "Buy of me gold tried in the fire" (v18). Gold speaks of the divine nature. In verse 21, Christ left them with this promise: "To him that overcometh will I grant to sit with me in my throne, even as I also overcame, and am set down with my Father in his throne." The key word here is *"overcometh."*

We are the sons of David

Most Christians recognize themselves as the spiritual offspring of Abraham. We are called to inherit the same blessings of Abraham. Abraham represents fruitfulness and fatherhood. He is called "the father of many nations." And while we are mentioning Abraham, Abraham was also a priest. He lived 500 years before the law. He was also of the regal calling (Gen. 23:6, 17:6). We, his children, are called to follow in the steps of faithful Abraham. (See Rom. 4:12)

We claim our heritage to Abraham through faith in Christ, who is also a son of Abraham. Spiritual circumcision of heart makes us true sons. However, we should take note of Matthew 1:1: "The book of the generation of Jesus Christ, *the son of David,* the son of Abraham." It is not just the son of Abraham, but also, "the son of David." David is the ruling family of Abraham's seed. We are also sons of David through faith as we also walk the spiritual walk of David.

David's Tabernacle represents those who have ascended the mountain—those who have overcome and are reigning. God will have a group that comes out of His Church that have reigned and will reign! "And she brought forth a man child, who was to rule all nations with a rod of iron: and her child was caught up unto God, and to his throne" (Rev.12:5). Although there are other interpretations of this verse, clearly, here is a group that comes out of the Church that knows the reality of sitting with Christ in heavenly places.

"And saviours [or deliverers] shall come up on mount Zion to judge the mount of Esau; and the kingdom shall be the LORD'S" (Obad.1:21). There will be those within the kingdom that inherit the birthright, and those who sell their birthrights. Those who come up to spiritual Zion shall reign over those who have forfeited their birthrights. See Matthew 25:28, Luke 19:26.

Psalm 149 - The reigning Church

> (Psa 149:5)
> "Let the saints be joyful in glory: let them sing aloud upon their beds."

(Psa 149:6)
"Let the high praises of God be in their mouth, and a two-edged sword in their hand."

(Psa 149:7)
"To execute vengeance upon the heathen, and punishments upon the people."

(Psa 149:8)
"To bind their kings with chains, and their nobles with fetters of iron."

(Psa 149:9)
"To execute upon them the judgment written: this honour have all his saints."

Psalm 149 is directed to the children of Zion. Note the word "saints." Paul said we are "called to be saints." Sainthood is worked out in our lives as we yield to the Spirit. If we want to rule the nations, we must first be overcomers.

CHAPTER SEVEN

The Higher Worship of Mount Zion

As we have affirmed in past lessons, David's Tabernacle brought in a whole new order to Israel. The services conducted before this tent broke all of the traditions. This tabernacle was setting a new precedent for the coming Church Age. In this chapter we are going to consider the higher form of worship upon Mount Zion in its various forms and expressions.

Costly worship

"And they sung as it were a new song before the throne, and before the four beasts, and the elders:

and no man could learn that song but the hundred and forty and four thousand, which were redeemed from the earth" (Rev.14:3). Here is a scene of the Mount Zion in heaven, and here is a group of people that are singing a song that cannot be learned in the ages to come. I think that it is clear from other passages in the book of Revelation that there are dimensions of glory that cannot be attained to in the next life. For example, in chapter fifteen, there is a group standing on the sea of glass mingled with fire. They are singing the song of Moses the servant of God, and the song of the Lamb.

Who can sing this song?

Moses symbolized the Old Testament. He was called the *meekest* man on the face of the earth. Christ symbolized the New Covenant and He was the *meekest* man of all time. Who are the people that can sing the Song of Moses and the Song of the Lamb?—only those who have learned meekness. One cannot sing a song in heaven that they have refused to learn upon earth. "These are they which follow the Lamb whithersoever he goeth" (Rev. 14:4). True Zion worship represents a very costly production, a sacrifice of a sweet savor to God. It can only be produced by those who have followed the Lamb with their whole heart. David said: "My soul followeth hard after thee" (Psa. 63:8).

I think one of the greatest examples of a true worshipper is exemplified by Mary of Bethany. "Then took Mary a pound of ointment of spikenard, very costly, and anointed the feet of Jesus, and wiped his feet with her hair: and the house was filled with the odour of the ointment" (John 12:3). True worship has the sense of kissing the feet of the one you love. The ointment used by Mary was worth a whole year's wages.

Praise waits for Thee in Sion - Psalm 65:1

There is a difference between praise and worship. There are many expressions of praise or laudation. They are expressions of the soul. David said, "bless the Lord O my soul *and let all that is within me* bless his holy name." That does not sound like someone who is passively sitting on the pew with his mouth closed.

When David planted his tabernacle on Mount Zion, he introduced a new range to the worship department. He appointed ministries to minister before the Ark. "And he appointed certain of the Levites to minister before the Ark of the LORD, and to record, and to thank and praise the LORD God of

Israel" (1 Chron.16:4). This was certainly a new thing!

"God inhabits the praises of his people" (Psa. 22:3). The word "inhabit" has the sense of pouncing on the prey as would a lion. God loves true worship and "pounces" upon it quickly! However, I say *true* worship because some churches think the Lord is so desperate for attention that He will accept any kind of worship. I attended such a church in the past. The mentality there was that worship would erase and excuse all of their sins and carnality. Actually, it is quite incredible how some people can worship for hours and then go off and continue their sinful lifestyles.

* Note: I am using the word *worship* to incorporate all of the expressions of adulation, praise, and worship. I will expound upon the terms individually a little later.

The Lord Discriminates

The Lord is very discriminating about the worship He receives. In fact, there is an account in the Law where two of Aaron's sons, Nadab and Abihu, offered strange fire or strange incense to the Lord. Both of them died before the Lord. (See Leviticus 10:1.) There is a lot of strange incense being offered up to the Lord today, but it is still unacceptable and it still brings spiritual death. David Wilkerson made this point very clear when he told a story about a church where "Christian" rock was being played. He said that when the music started, there were puffs of smoke released from the stage, and in those puffs of smoke he saw forms of demons.

All of that worship was being received by demonic spirits, and this was being promoted on God's altar. Instead of being released from their bondages, the cheering Christians were being strengthened in their bondages. Instead of God being glorified, Satan was being lifted up. How do you think God feels about this?

True worshippers

Paul said, "We are the circumcision that worship God in the spirit, and rejoice in Christ Jesus, and have no confidence in the flesh" (Phil. 3:3). Only those who experience true circumcision in their hearts can worship in the Spirit. Circumcision of heart is the cutting away of the old nature with which we were born, the flesh. "But the hour cometh, and now is, when the true worshippers shall worship the Father in spirit and in truth: for the Father seeketh such to worship him" (John 4:23).

Davidic worship

This thought of "Davidic worship" can be appreciated more by studying the later revivals. For example, the revival that took place during King Hezekiah's reign *reinstituted* all of the Davidic order of worship. This was about 300 years after David. Hezekiah set in place all of the Levitical musicians, the singers, the Davidic instruments, and the courses to thank and to praise the Lord. These were the same Levitical families that David had appointed centuries before. (See 2 Chronicles 29:25-30.)

Names like *Asaph, Heman, and Jeduthun* became "guild" names. Their ministry passed down to the descending generations. You could well see the name Asaph on a Psalm that was written long after the original Asaph. Please understand that these were not the same people, but they were of the same family.

The revivalists always came back to the Davidic order of worship, not the Mosaic order. Even today we are just getting back to the original pattern of David. The worship that we find in the Psalms has never ceased to be acceptable. The reason that many of God's people say it cannot be justified in the New Testament is because they have failed to reckon with Acts chapter fifteen. "After this I will return, and will build again the tabernacle of David, which is fallen down; and I will build again the ruins thereof, and I will set it up" (Acts 15:16).

Various expressions of praise and worship:
(These will be in summary)
Lifting hands

- Psalm 63:4

"I will lift up my hands in thy name." (This expression to God is mentioned often.)

- Psalm 134:2

" Lift up your hands in the sanctuary, and bless the LORD."

- Lamentations 3:41

"Let us lift up our heart with our hands unto God in the heavens."

- Psalm 141:2

"Let my prayer be set forth before thee as incense; and the lifting up of my hands as the evening sacrifice."

Lifting up of the hands expresses many things. It can be an expression of faith when we pray. It can symbolize surrendering our heart. It can be an extension of worship or blessing. When Moses held up his hands, the enemy was defeated. It can also symbolize reliance upon God. Any of these expressions of lifting the hands can be powerful when they are in sync with the Spirit of God! Someone had a vision once of a cloud of incense going up as the people were lifting their hands.

Clapping the hands

Psalm 47:1 - "O clap your hands, all ye people." Clapping the hands is a declaration of jubilation and victory, as it was in this Psalm. It can also be a demonstration of judgment against the enemy (cf. Ezk. 21:17). A vision was once shared about a congregation that was clapping triumphantly, and that clapping was actually buffeting the demonic powers that were trying to subdue them. Thus, the clapping of hands can be a weapon against our enemies.

Dancing

Psalm 149:3 - "Let them praise his name in the dance." The Lord is extolled in the dance. When the Ark came into Jerusalem, the congregation was dancing, and the only one who was offended by this was smitten with barrenness (2 Sam. 6:14-23)! When Jesus made His triumphal entry into

Jerusalem, there was dancing. When the prodigal son returned, there was dancing. When Israel is restored in the last days, there will be dancing!

Let me share a story about a friend of mine who attended a Bible school up in the Adirondack mountains. In 1974, as the school was dismissing for term break, the president of the school said, "I had an unusual vision of Jesus dancing in the midst of his people." When the next term began, the dancing began. There was such an outbreak of joy that it could not be contained. The students danced through the whole semester and then it ended as abruptly as it had started. Incidentally, the dancing is before the Lord, not with one another. One might ask, "What did it accomplish?" It brought unity, healing, and a release of the spiritual gifts. It brought an impartation of blessings that most Christians never see.

Rejoicing

Psalm 149:2 - "Let Israel rejoice in him that made him: let the children of Zion be joyful in their King." Here again is an expression of the soul that has many variations. Some of them could include leaping, and spinning about. (See number 1523 in the "Strong's" Hebrew concordance).

There are times when the spirit of rejoicing

comes, but there are other times when we must stir ourselves to rejoice. The enemy cannot stand before those who are rejoicing in their God. Mount Zion is a place of rejoicing. Incidentally, the original Greek word used for *rejoice* at the marriage supper of the Lamb means "to leap for joy" (Rev.19:7).

* Note: Sometimes the word "joyful" transliterates into the same Hebrew word as *rejoice*. [e. g.] *"Rejoice* greatly, O daughter of Zion" (Zec. 9:9). "Let the children of Zion be *joyful* in their King" (Psa.149:2).

Hebrew Concordance # 1523 — *giyl;* or (by perm.) *guwl*; a prim. root; prop. to spin round (under the influence of any violent emotion), Both words are 1523 in the Hebrew.

Shouting

Psalm 47:1 - "Shout unto God with the voice of triumph." The expression, "shout for joy" is used on numerous occasions in the Psalms. Shouting can also be a legitimate manifestation of praise to God. Shouting, like any other form of exultation, can bring release in the Spirit. The walls of Jericho came down with a shout! God's people were in tune with heaven.

Praise

Psalm 50:23 - "Whoso offereth praise glorifieth me." It is interesting that the word *praise* is only used seven times until the time of David. The Psalms record the word <u>praise</u> 160 times. The word <u>praise</u>, basically means "to extol, or glorify the Lord." It is generally expressed by singing, shouting, or playing instruments. Many people do not realize how destitute the Church world was during the Dark Ages. There were no instruments in the Church. There was no song in the Church of the Dark Ages—perhaps only a chant, or a slow mournful funeral hymn or lament.

Singing

The word *"sing"* is used at least seventy times in the Psalms. Singing is one of the most powerful forms of praise and adulation. In fact, battles have been won by singing, even as Jehoshaphat's battle with the mixed multitude: "And when he had consulted with the people, he appointed *singers* unto the LORD, and that should praise the beauty of holiness, as they went out before the army, and to say, Praise the LORD; for his mercy endureth for ever. And when they began to *sing* and to praise, the LORD set ambushments against the children of Ammon, Moab, and mount

Seir, which were come against Judah; and they were smitten" (2 Chr. 20:21-22).

Paul and Silas sang praises from the inner prison at midnight. Talk about bringing release! Their chains fell off, their stocks fell off, and the prison doors opened up. They actually released a revival in the prison by singing praises. (See Acts 16:24-30.)

Thanksgiving

Psalm 100:4 - "Enter into his gates with thanksgiving." This Psalm gives us the correct format to approach our God. Thanksgiving is one of the essentials of the worship service. Thanksgiving is mentioned about 30 times in the Psalms. Giving thanks to the Lord releases faith. Paul said to make our supplications known to God with thanksgiving. We are thanking Him in advance! (See Phil. 4:6.)

David appointed courses of Levites to give thanks. It was part of the service. (See 1 Chr. 16:4, 35; 23:30; 25:3.) Testimony services are always nice. But it is also nice when the thanksgiving comes spontaneously, perhaps during an interlude in the song service. I have even noticed at times a prophetic impulse as people gave thanks for things yet to be! Thanksgiving can create an atmosphere for the Spirit of God to move.

Laughing

Psalm 126:2 - "Then was our mouth filled with laughter." Laughter is another expression of victory or triumph. The Scripture says: "He that sitteth in the heavens shall laugh." This passage is referring to Christ in Psalm 2:4. However, David penned this Psalm as he sat upon Mount Zion and as the Lord gave him the dominion over his enemies. I believe David experienced "sitting in heavenly places" far above his enemies. David experienced the "holy laughter" of triumph.

I was once in a country where the Church had experienced a real breakthrough in the Spirit. At times this church would experience waves of laughter, which brought physical healing to many. "A merry heart doeth good like a medicine" (Prov.17:22). Laughing can be a witness of the Spirit of God!

Davidic instruments

1 Chronicles 23:5 - "And four thousand praised the LORD with the instruments which I made, said David, to praise therewith." As we have previously noted, the later revivals all came back to the Davidic instruments and worship. These are some of the instruments you will find associated with David:

- Flutes
- Cornets
- Varied pitched harps
- Varied stringed instruments
- Varied pitched cymbals
- Timbrels
- Psalteries
- Organs (wind-reed instruments)
- Trumpets

In 1 Chronicles 23:5, there is a strong emphasis on David's instruments. Sometimes there are problems associated with instruments. The percussion section can be a problem. The wrong beat or rhythm can taint the worship. In some cases it brings in the wrong spirit. Getting the paganistic mixture out of the worship is a major concern on the mission field. I was once in one of these primitive village churches where the drummer was beating on a barrel. There was no anointing upon their worship.

Drums can be legitimate in the right setting. The Salvation Army band playing militant or marching type of anthems can actually be quite inspiring. Snare drums building up to a crescendo in certain exultations can be very anointed.

Obviously, there are many more instruments around in our twentieth and twenty-first centuries. Yet our main concern is that they produce the same anointing as David's instruments. The minor key can drag the service down, perhaps causing a depressing mood. Of course, this is not always the case. We need to divide soul from spirit in our music departments. This is illustrated below:

The Musical Scale

In Pastor James Shaffer's book on Bible Numerics and Music, he explains some of the numerical vibrations on the piano. He also shows how that the musical scale reveals the seven dispensations:

C-major   –   The creation
D-minor   –   The fall of Adam
E-minor   –   The flood
F-major   –   The birth and ministry of Christ
G-major   –   The birth of the Church
                  (Pentecost)
A-minor   –   The anti-christ reign
B-diminished –   The Millennial reign (There is
                  still sin in the Millennium.)
C-major   –   The new heaven, and the new
                  earth. (The eighth note is the same
                  as the first note, only a complete
                  octave higher. The new heaven
                  and earth is greater than the Eden
                  creation.)

What this scale shows us is that we do not want to major in the minor!

*Note: Many of the Psalm headings are set with Hebrew terms, which are, in effect, musical terminology. They give the mood, and the instruments with which the Psalm was to be put to music.

Worship

Psalm 99:5 - "... Exalt ye the LORD our God, and worship at his footstool; for he is holy. Psalm 95:6 – "O come, let us worship and bow down: let us kneel before the LORD our maker." There is a certain procedure to come into His presence. The outer court represents thanksgiving and praise. But worship, in its truest form, is what takes place before His throne. When the Lord is coming down the street there is jubilation, rejoicing, and dancing, but when the Lord is on his throne the order changes to worship. Worship has the sense of falling upon our face.

In many of the churches of our fellowship, it is common to see people bowing or kneeling, or even lying prostrate. True worship is absolute surrender. In the garden of Gethsemane man had to fall *backward* in the presence of the "I Am." After Christ was resurrected, His disciples fell at His feet in worship. (Compare John 18:6 and Matthew 28:9.)

It is in the true expression of worship that we are changed. We are "changed into His image as we behold Him" (11 Cor. 3:18). We are changed from glory to glory in this place of worship. The Psalmist said we become *like* the object of our affection. (See Psalm 135:18.)

In conclusion of this chapter, let me again recall the verses in 2 Chronicles 1:3-4. "And all the congregation with him, went to the high place that was at Gibeon; for there was the tabernacle of the congregation of God, which Moses the servant of the LORD had made in the wilderness. But the Ark of God had David brought up from Kirjathjearim to the place which David had prepared for it: for he had pitched a tent for it at Jerusalem." The Ark was in the Tabernacle of David.

The golden altar moves within the veil

In his explanation of Moses' tabernacle, the Apostle Paul takes the liberty of moving the golden altar from the holy place into the holy of holies: "And after the second veil, the tabernacle which is called the Holiest of all; Which had the golden censer, and the Ark of the covenant overlaid round about with gold" (Heb. 9:3-4). Paul actually moves the golden altar within the veil, by the Spirit. The altar was always on "this side" of the veil. The golden altar speaks of prayer and praise. Do you see the significance? The New Testament calling is to minister *within* the veil!

The worshippers at Gibeon were going through the legitimate forms of worship in the outer court, yet the object of their worship, symbolized in the Ark, was in the Tabernacle of David upon the holy hill in Jerusalem. We will later consider David's question: "Who shall ascend into the hill of the Lord?" This is an important question, because the answer shows us the qualifications for abiding in God's presence.

CHAPTER EIGHT

The Music Department of David's Tabernacle

Music is one of the significant dimensions of David's Tabernacle. As previously stated, David brought in a new era of music and song, setting a precedent for the Church. In this chapter we are going to consider the divinely appointed musicians and the ministry of music.

The effects of music

Before we look at the music department of David, let us consider some of the effects that music has in the realm of the Spirit:

Music brings the presence of the Lord

As you will recall, it was the musicians and singers that ushered in the presence of the Lord to Mount Zion. "…The singers went before, the players on instruments followed after" (Psa. 68:24-25). This is in reference to the procession that ushered in the Ark. Anointed music brings the Spirit of God. In the last few decades there has been a fresh inspiration on Scripture songs. Literally thousands of verses have been put to music and are sung in the churches. When these passages are in tune with what the Spirit is saying, they are very powerful and they bring the presence of the Lord.

Music brings deliverance and healing

When King Saul was oppressed by evil spirits, his servants found an anointed musician, whose playing drove away the demons. Saul was healed by David's anointed fingers. David said: "Blessed be the LORD my strength, which teacheth my hands to war, and my fingers to fight" (Psa.144:1). Even the ladies can fight against the enemy with their anointed fingers! "And it came to pass, when the evil spirit from God was upon Saul, that David took an harp, and played with his hand: so Saul was refreshed, and was well, and the evil spirit departed from him" (I Sam.16:23).

Music brings the prophetic Word

When Elisha was seeking for a fresh word from God concerning the battle between King Jehoshaphat and the Moabites, he sought for a minstrel. "But now bring me a minstrel. And it came to pass, when the minstrel played, that the hand of the LORD came upon him" (2 Kgs. 3:11-19). The anointed minstrel released the word of the Lord. Never underestimate the power of anointed music. Even today most prophetic utterances come during the musical interlude of the worship service. In fact, many of the gifts of the Spirit are released through the musical part of the service.

As you will see later on in this study, the Levitical musicians were not just skillful players, but *prophetic* musicians. Samuel raised up many prophetic minstrels. David must have picked up some of Samuel's mantle.

Anointed music brings conviction

Although this thought might be a little more difficult to define from Scripture, most Christians will agree that the *"altar call"* music affects the sinner more than the sermon affects him. When Saul sent messengers to seek after David, they came into the company of the prophetic musicians and the

Spirit of God fell upon them also. Saul was actually slain by the Spirit. (See 1 Samuel 19:20-24.)

1 Samuel 10:5-6 - "Thou shalt meet with a psaltery a company of prophets coming down from the high place, and a tabret, and a pipe, and a harp, before them; and they shall prophesy: And the spirit of the LORD will come upon thee, and thou shalt prophesy with them, and shalt be turned into another man." Anointed music brings the Spirit of the Lord, and with the Spirit of the Lord comes great *conviction!*

The musicians can bring the cloud of glory

Such was the case in 2 Chronicles 5:12-14: "… Also the Levites which were the singers, all of them of Asaph, of Heman, of Jeduthun, with their sons and their brethren, being arrayed in white linen, having cymbals and psalteries and harps, stood at the east end of the altar, and with them an hundred and twenty priests sounding with trumpets: It came even to pass, as the trumpeters and singers were as one, to make one sound to be heard in praising and thanking the LORD; and when they lifted up their voice with the trumpets and cymbals and instruments of music, and praised the LORD, saying, For he is good; for his mercy endureth for ever: that then the house was filled with a cloud, even the house of the LORD; So that the priests could not stand to minister by reason of the cloud: for the glory of the LORD had filled the house of God."

As we realize the spiritual influences of music, we can also understand why Satan seeks to corrupt the music department. The *evil one* knows all about music and worship. He is the one who led worship in heaven. Ezekiel calls him "the anointed cherub" (Ezk. 28:14). Corrupted music will produce just the *reverse* of what we have studied in this chapter. Instead of deliverance, it will produce bondage, sickness, lasciviousness (loose living), false anointings, and false gifts.

The music department of David

Mount Zion speaks of the higher standard. That is why David organized his music department, setting a precedent for the Church. Mount Zion speaks of government, and it is here that David ordained twenty-four musical courses. These courses functioned at their appointed times throughout the year. Basically the appointments were to the chief musicians and their families. These appointments headed up the music team for their particular course.

There is coming a time of great blessing to the Church. Even though some of the smaller churches cannot appreciate this now, in the future there will be a need for various teams of players and leaders. We have attended churches that needed four worship leaders to cover the platform. It is interesting how different song leaders bring different flavors from the Lord. The tree of life had "twelve manner of fruit," one for every month of the year (Rev. 22:2).

This part of the study will help us to see the Scriptural authority for the *appointments* of music ministries, and will help us understand that these giftings come from God. We were once challenged by one of our congregants on the subject of "the worship leader." They said that the worship leader had no authority to tell the congregation to lift their hands or to clap their hands, etc. I pointed them to David's music ministers, and that seemed to resolve the conflict.

Even in the Psalms there are many responsive parts. For example, the sons of Korah were one of the branches of the music ministry. (See Psalm 47:1 and title.) At times a music leader might command the congregation to clap their hands. Not responding to the leader's exhortation would certainly be showing contempt.

Divine appointments

We must realize that these ministries were not just voted into place, but were placed there by prophetic unction. 1 Chronicles 9:22 states: "...Whom David and Samuel the seer did ordain in their set office." "And he set the Levites in the house of the LORD with cymbals, with psalteries, and with harps, according to the commandment of David, and of Gad the king's seer, and Nathan the prophet: for so was the commandment of the LORD by his prophets" (2 Chron. 29:25). As the Church enters into revival these truths will become very real!

R. Edward Miller, missionary to Argentina, tells a story about a pianist in his church who brought the presence of God as she played. However, there was also another accomplished pianist in his church with much talent. One day he decided to put the lady with all of the musical degrees on the church piano. He describes what followed as *a spiritual disaster!* The point is not how technically correct one's playing is, but whether God's approval and anointing is there!

Chenaniah, the master song leader (Jehovah empowers)

1 Chronicles 15:22,27 - "And Chenaniah, [a choral director] chief of the Levites, was for song: he instructed about the song, because he was skilful... And David was clothed with a robe of fine linen, and all the Levites that bare the Ark, and the

singers, and Chenaniah the master of the song with the singers." Here is the authority for the music director. Although there are many facets of the music department, there must be *one* who is orchestrating the program. The music department should be governed, either by David (the pastor), or a music director subject to the pastor—someone like Chenaniah.

Asaph, Heman, and Jeduthun

1 Chronicles 25:1 - Here are the three chief musicians. These three Levites represent the three families of Levi: (See Gen. 46:11.)

- *Asaph* represents the family of Gershon, the son of Levi.
- *Heman* represents the family of Kohath, the son of Levi. (Aaron's line also came from Kohath).
- *Jeduthun* represents the family of Merari, the son of Levi.

There are forty-five titles *"To the Chief Musician"* in the Psalms. Under these three chief musical directors were 288 skilled music instructors. Many of these included their own sons and daughters: (cf. 1 Chron. 25:6) - "All these were under the hands of their father for song in the house of the LORD, with cymbals, psalteries, and harps, for the service of the house of God, according to the king's order to Asaph, Jeduthun, and Heman."

1 Chronicles 25:7 - "So the number of them, with their brethren that were instructed in the songs of the LORD, even all that were cunning, was two hundred fourscore and eight." These 288 skilled musicians were then divided up into 24 groups of 12. Each one of these groups were to direct the 24 courses of Levite musicians. (See 1 Chron. 25:6-31.)

12 Speaks of government (twelve Apostles).
24 Speaks of government (twenty-four Elders).
288 Speaks of the combined government of the Church and Israel (144 x 2, cf. Rev. 7:4, 14:1).

The big picture

According to the Jewish historian Josephus, these 24 courses functioned on a two-week basis. And there were about 250 musicians in each course. On special occasions, such as the three main feasts of Israel, they could all be present. That could incorporate about 4000 players, plus the choral groups.

1 Chronicles 23:5 - "Moreover four thousand were [gate keepers]; and four thousand praised the LORD with the instruments which I made, said David, to praise therewith." You can visualize the joy of such a scene. Perhaps Psalm 87:6-7 expresses such an occasion: "The LORD shall count, when he writeth up the people, that this man was born there. Selah. As well the singers as the players on instruments shall be there."

*Note: Although there was a continual ministry before the Ark under the auspices of the chief musicians, the actual appointment of these 24 courses did not take place until the end of David's reign. They were never were put into full motion until after the temple was built. (cf. 2 Chr. 5:11).

What we must see is that David ordained his governmental structure during the *Mount Zion order.* The government is later brought down to the temple. Solomon's Temple is a figure of the finished church. We will consider this later.

Prophetic musicians

1 Chronicles 25:1 - "Moreover David and the captains of the host separated to the service of the sons of Asaph, and of Heman, and of Jeduthun, who should prophesy with harps, with psalteries, and with cymbals." One thing that we come to appreciate

about the Davidic era is that it was a very prophetic era. Prophecy just flowed from the music department. Their anointed playing brought the spirit of prophecy. The Apostle Paul said to seek for the prophetic flow in your life. (See 1 Cor.14:1). I believe that the Church finale shall be very prophetic.

Asaph (he restores)

Although these three chief musicians were skillful on all the instruments; they all seem to have their special emphasis. Asaph was known for his *cymbals* (cf. 1 Chron.16:5). And as we have already stated, he was a prophetic player as well. "…The sons of Asaph under the hands of Asaph, which prophesied according to the order of the king" (1 Chron. 25:2).

The name of Asaph became a guild name to the whole family line. Also the music mantle and the prophetic mantle stayed upon the Asaphites for centuries. Many of the Psalms that are entitled *"A Psalm of Asaph"* were written centuries after the "original" Asaph. Psalms 73 through 83 are all Asaph Psalms.

We see a beautiful picture of this prophetic mantle During the time of Jehoshaphat. This event took place perhaps 150 years after the "Asaph" of David's time. King Jehoshaphat was facing a battle with a number of confederate nations. As he gathered his congregation for prayer in the court of the Lord, the Spirit of the Lord came upon one of the sons of Asaph. "Then upon Jahaziel the son of Zechariah, the son of Benaiah, the son of Jeiel, the son of Mattaniah, a Levite of the sons of Asaph, came the Spirit of the LORD in the midst of the congregation" (2 Chron. 20:14).

This son of Asaph then prophesied the victorious outcome of the battle. Do you see how this beautiful mantle of prophecy flowed down through the spiritual descendents? Asaph's children also ministered during the Restoration Era.

This is one of the reasons why we in the Church Age want to meet with God. There is a spiritual endowment to be gained. When Jacob wrestled with the Lord, he knew there was more to the blessing than just a good feeling or some tangible substance. He knew that the spiritual endowment would affect the forth-coming generations.

Heman (faithful)

Heman was of the Kohath line, a grandson of the prophet Samuel. One can easily understand the prophetic mantle upon this musician because of his relationship to the great prophet (1 Chr. 6:33). Heman is actually called *"the king's seer."* A seer is a prophet. "All these were the sons of Heman the king's seer in the words of God, to lift up the horn. And God gave to Heman fourteen sons and three daughters" (1 Chr. 25:5). You will also note in this verse, that his emphasis was on the *horn*. These instruments can bring such a beautiful presence of God when they are anointed. I have seen the clouds of glory appear when the trumpeter was sounding.

The word of the Lord was still flowing out of this family guild 400 years later. We will see these three families still flowing in the ministry during Josiah's revival.

Jeduthun (praise)

Jeduthun and Ethan are thought to be the same person. Jeduthun is particularly known for his harp section. "Of Jeduthun: the sons of Jeduthun; Gedaliah, and Zeri, and Jeshaiah, Hashabiah, and Mattithiah, six, under the hands of their father Jeduthun, *who prophesied with a harp,* to give thanks and to praise the LORD" (1 Chron. 25:3). Once again, here is a very anointed family who led the congregation into praise and thanksgiving. Jeduthun's name is found in three of the Psalm headings—Psalms 39, 62, and 77. This is also a very prophetic family.

The harpists in heaven mentioned in the book of

Revelation make up a very exclusive group of musicians (cf. Rev.14:2). They have been given the right to play in this group because they have overcome in this life. Their lives have been a praise unto His glory. Josephus mentions the same type of harp mentioned of in Revelation, a ten stringed harp. The *number ten* speaks of the law, and those who play these harps have fulfilled the law. "Praise the LORD with harp: sing unto him with the psaltery and an instrument of *ten* strings" (Psa. 33:2).

Spiritual seed

In conclusion of this chapter, I want to re-emphasize the truth of *"spiritual descendents."* The Levite ministers passed on a spiritual mantle to their offspring. That truth is an example to us! Unless we impart something of spiritual substance to our children (natural children or spiritual children), then all of the promises will die with us! Inheritance always involves our seed.

That is why we as ministers need to meet with God to receive that spiritual endowment, so that the promises and the blessings we receive can be imparted to our children. Take, for example, the promise that God made to Joshua, that no man could stand against him. This same promise came upon his congregation. Compare Joshua 1:5 with Joshua 23:9.

"There shall not any man be able to stand before *thee* all the days of thy life" (Josh. 1:5) "For the LORD hath driven out from before you great nations and strong: but as for you, no man hath been able to stand before *you* unto this day" (Josh. 23:9).

Let us consider another verse: "As for me, this is my covenant with them, saith the LORD; My spirit that is upon thee, and my words which I have put in thy mouth, shall not depart out of thy mouth, nor out of the mouth of thy seed, nor out of the mouth of thy seed's seed, saith the LORD, from henceforth and for ever" (Isa 59:21).

CHAPTER NINE

Courses of Ministry Established Under The Mount Zion Order

I n chapter nine, we will see the governmental structure being set up under the *Mount Zion order*. We are going to consider the priestly courses and how they could have application today. We will also consider some of the other courses of ministry and see their relevance for the Church today. This new government came into full recognition after Solomon's temple was completed.

Understanding the purpose of the Mt. Zion order

In order to understand the concept of the tent on Mount Zion, let us consider two different scenarios. First, picture Jerusalem in the time of David with its two mountains. One is Mount Zion, where David ordains those who will administrate the forth-coming order. The other mount is Moriah, where the temple will be built. Once that temple comes into place, the new administration brings the Ark down from David's Tabernacle into the temple. Now the glory of God fills the temple, and the new government is in motion.

Although Mount Zion is the higher place and speaks of the ultimate position in Christ, it has now fulfilled its purpose (in a figure) by drawing upward those men and women of the true vision. "...Every one of them in Zion appeareth before God" (Psa. 84:7). Those who have met with God in Zion are coming down to the temple, and they are endued with power and glory! They are bearing the Ark, and the temple is the final destination of the Ark. It is here that the staves used for carrying the Ark are finally removed (2 Chr. 5:9).

The second picture is an anti-type of the first. Those who have apprehended the high calling of God in Christ, those who have experienced the New Covenant reality, those who are indeed seated with

Christ in heavenly places are those who will bear His presence into the Church of the last day. The Church is also called "the temple of his body." It will be finished, and it will be glorified.

The Church of Jesus Christ must come to completeness. The Lord declared that He would build His Church and be glorified in it (Mt. 16:18, cf. Eph. 5:27). Solomon's Temple pictures how *the last day Church* will finish. It is completed and it is filled with the glory of God as it ushers in the next dispensation. The Solomon era is a type of the Millennial age, a reign of peace and blessing.

The twenty-four priestly courses
(See 1 Chronicles 24:1-19.)

As you will see in 1 Chronicles 24:1-19, the twenty-four courses of *priests* were also ordained by divine appointment. David appointed these courses by "lot." Casting lots was legitimate when in the hands of the ordained leadership. The Lord determines the outcome of the *lot.* "The lot is cast into the lap; but the whole disposing thereof is of the LORD" (Prov. 16:33). These twenty-four appointments would be in charge of the course for their particular weeks of service. We should also note that the mantle of these appointments was to be handed down to the succeeding families. Twenty-four can speak of eldership (cf.

Rev. 4:4, 4:10). There are twenty-four elders around the throne.

John the Baptist's course

Luke 1:5, 8 - "There was in the days of Herod, the king of Judaea, a certain priest named Zacharias, *of the course of Abia:* and his wife was of the daughters of Aaron, and her name was Elisabeth. And it came to pass, that while he executed the priest's office before God in the order of his course..." Zacharias the priest was functioning in the same course that David had set into motion 1000 years earlier— "The seventh to Hakkoz, *the eighth to Abijah*" (1 Chr. 24:10). Abia, and Abijah are the same. Zacharias was the father of John the Baptist, making John of that same priestly course. John obviously was given a very different kind of course, which he fulfilled (Acts 13:25).

Two lines of priests

All of the priests had to come from Aaron's line. Aaron originally had four sons, but two of them died before the Lord for offering strange incense (Lev.10:1,2). That left two lines through which the priests could come—either from Eleazar or Ithamar. Let us consider the following verse: "And there were more chief men found of the sons of Eleazar than of the sons of Ithamar; and thus were they divided. Among the sons of Eleazar there were *sixteen* chief men of the house of their fathers, and *eight* among the sons of Ithamar according to the house of their fathers" (1 Chr. 24:4). Twice as many came from Eleazar's line (16 men) compared to Ithamar's (8 men).

I think this is a very important point. These two families of Aaron had continued about 500 years, and by the time that David divided these courses, there could have been a high priest from either side. In David's time, *Abiathar* represented the family of Ithamar, the son of Aaron, and *Zadok* represented Eleazar, the son of Aaron. By the end of David's reign these two lines become very clear. Abiathar the high priest joins with Adonijah who is trying to usurp the throne, but Zadok remains faithful to David (cf. 1 Kings 1). The end of David's reign and life symbolizes the end of the Church Age, and these two lines of priests symbolize *two streams of ministry* within the Church.

The Zadok line becomes dominant during the Mount Zion order

It almost seems that Abiathar's line was doomed to fail in fulfillment of the word spoken against Eli's house. (Eli was in the Ithamar line. See 1 Samuel 3:27-36.) In the end the faithful sons of Zadok will have the dominant ministry. The difference was two to one! Zadok had the double portion. Ezekiel elaborates upon the Zadok priesthood quite extensively in chapter 44. Incidentally, Ezekiel himself was a Zadokite.

Sixteen courses came from the Zadok line, whereas only eight came from the Abiathar line. The sons of Zadok are given the privilege of *ministering to the Lord.* The other priests can only *minister to the people* in the outer court. That makes all the difference! Let's read this in Ezekiel 44:11-15.

Ezekiel 44:11-15 - "Yet they shall be ministers in my sanctuary, having charge at the gates of the house, and *ministering to the house:* they shall slay the burnt offering and the sacrifice for the people, and they shall stand before them to minister unto them. Because they ministered unto them before their idols, and caused the house of Israel to fall into iniqsuity; therefore have I lifted up mine hand against them, saith the Lord God, and they shall bear their iniquity. And they shall not come near unto me, to do the office of a priest unto me, nor to come near to any of my holy things in the most holy place: but they shall bear their shame, and their abominations which they have committed. But I will make them keepers of the charge of the house, for all the service thereof, and for all that shall be done therein. But the priests the Levites, the sons of Zadok, that kept the charge of my sanctuary when the children of Israel went astray from me, *they shall come near to me to minister unto me,* and they shall stand before me to offer unto me the fat and the blood, saith the Lord GOD.

The priestly ministry

Although the priestly functions varied as to their particular duties, their basic functions were in the areas of mediation, or intercession. The priest burned incense before the Lord. Burning incense speaks of intercessory prayer. The table of shew-bread of which he tended represents the pure word, and the ministry of the word to God's people.

I think the prophet Malachi expresses the call and ministry of Levi very well: "And ye shall know that I have sent this commandment unto you, that my covenant might be with Levi, saith the LORD of hosts. My covenant was with him of life and peace; and I gave them to him for the fear wherewith he feared me, and was afraid before my name. The law of truth was in his mouth, and iniquity was not found in his lips: he walked with me in peace and equity, *and did turn many away from iniquity*" (Mal. 2:4-6).

"He turned many from iniquity." This is where the house of Eli failed. Eli was full of compromise and

partiality in judgment. The priest was not only to teach God's standard, but his life was to be the standard. For example, consider Ezra the priest: "For Ezra had prepared his heart to seek the law of the LORD, *and to do it,* and to teach in Israel statutes and judgments" (Ezra 7:10). Ezra practiced what he preached.

Malachi continues: *"For the priest's lips should keep knowledge, and they should seek the law at his mouth: for he is the messenger of the LORD of hosts"* (Mal. 2:7). The priest's lips should be filled with the knowledge of God. He hears from God. His message is from God. He is the messenger of the Lord of Hosts. When people come to the minister for counsel or direction, they want to hear what God has to say. Counsel is one of the seven Spirits of God. These seven anointings are typified by the candlestick with seven lamps which the priest was to attend to. Today, many ministers get into psychology or take courses on how to counsel various problems. However, true counsel comes from heaven, and there is no way that one can apply Bible principles to any given situation unless God is speaking it.

The teaching priest

*Note: Although we may seem to be going away from our subject, David's Tabernacle represents a covering that all the nations seek unto (cf. Acts 15:16-17). David's Tabernacle represents a group that shall teach the nations and bring a covering to them through the instrumentality of the *Word.* The Word creates a covering. The enemy seeks to attack those who are not strong in the Word or those who have been poorly taught.

Just to appreciate the effectiveness of the "teaching priest," consider the prosperity and peace that came upon the kingdom during the reign of King Jehoshaphat. Nations were afraid of Judah. The economy was flourishing, and it was all because the godly king had sent the priests throughout the cities to teach God's laws and judgments! (See 11 Chr.17:8-13.)

When we consider the great commission of Christ to teach all nations, it is obvious that the Church is farther from that commission than it was during the first century. "And this gospel of the kingdom shall be preached in all the world for a witness unto all nations; and then shall the end come" (Mt. 24:14). In the tabernacle of Moses, the holy place dimensions of 2000 represents the Church Age. The Church Age technically began about 30 AD. on the Day of Pentecost. Theoretically, that leaves about 30 years remaining for this age. Therefore, knowing the briefness of the time, there must be a tremendous revival in our day in order to fulfill the great commission.

The prophet Isaiah pictures the last day Church as a teaching Church: " And it shall come to pass in the last days, that the mountain of the Lord's house shall be established in the top of the mountains, and shall be exalted above the hills; and all nations shall flow unto it. And many people shall go and say, Come ye, and let us go up to the mountain of the LORD, to the house of the God of Jacob; and he will teach us of his ways, and we will walk in his paths: for out of Zion shall go forth the law, and the word of the LORD from Jerusalem" (Isa. 2:2-3). The nations will turn to the Church for the answers (cf. Isa. 60:1-3).

Indeed we realize that the *literal* interpretation of this verse is for Israel in the Millennium. However, the last-day Church must usher in this truth first because they precede the promises given to Israel. For example, the promise of the New Covenant in Jeremiah 31:31-34 was given to Israel, but as a nation, they will not enter that covenant until the Church Age is over because of their rejection of Christ. Nevertheless, the book of Hebrews declares the New Covenant to be valid to the Church because the veil has been rent.

John 7:37-38 - " In the last day, that great day of the feast, Jesus stood and cried saying, If any man thirst, let him come unto me, and drink. He that believeth on me, as the scripture hath said, out of his belly shall flow rivers of living water." In these passages Jesus is actually spiritualizing on the Millennial Temple spoken of in Ezekiel chapter 47.

In the Millennium there will be a literal temple with a literal river of water flowing out from Jerusalem. Jesus is applying this truth to our individual lives and to the Church as a whole. The point is, He is applying a Millennial truth to the Church Age. It is also interesting to note that during this last great Feast of Tabernacles, Christ emerges in the Temple as *The Teacher.* "Now about the midst of the feast Jesus went up into the temple, and taught. And the Jews marvelled, saying, How knoweth this man letters, having never learned?" (John 7:14-15)

"We need teachers"

In these last days there shall be an emergence of teachers. Those who have come up to Mount Zion shall now come down to teach the nations. Or if you prefer, the nations shall seek for the teacher. As we travel through various parts of the world, the cry is always the same: "We need teachers... send us teachers!" As a matter of fact, just this week (as I am writing this) we had a surprise visit from an African minister who said, "We need teachers!" The cry to "come over and help us" is being sounded in many places today (cf. Acts 16:9).

Ezra the Priest, of Zadok's line, raised up many teachers who came forward during the Feast of Tabernacles. Actually, twenty-six of Ezra's teachers are mentioned by name. The Feast of Tabernacles is to the end-time Church what Pentecost was to the early Church, only greater. (See Nehemiah Chapter 8 for the revival that was taking place during the Feast of Tabernacles).

The priestly course for our life
(We are a royal priesthood.)

Coming back to our original thought of the priestly courses, I believe that there will be courses of New Testament priests who will teach the nations, and thus fulfill the Great Commission.

Samuel traveled a circuit: "And he went from year to year in circuit to Bethel, and Gilgal, and Mizpeh, and judged Israel in all those places" (1 Sam. 7:16). As God develops a ministry within our lives, we could very well find ourselves on a yearly circuit or course. I have found this to be true in my own experience. Every year I find myself in certain countries and in certain Bible schools and churches, and every year the course seems to be lengthening. I also see this happening in the lives of many of my colleagues.

Our personal course

As New Testament priests, we go through our regular priestly duties every day, offering the spiritual sacrifices. (See chapter 5) Yet, I believe there comes a span of time in our lives when we begin our "course" or life's work. The course I am referring to now is that special task or purpose for which we were born. Perhaps you have been in the ministry for years and yet you know in your heart that you have not yet fulfilled the purpose for your existence. I believe that God takes us through many preliminary runs first to condition us for "the real shot." But before that happens, God spends many years preparing us to meet Him. Somehow it is in this meeting with God, even as Moses met God at the burning bush, that we are changed and we find ourselves on the "course."

Psalm 84:7 - "They go from strength to strength, every one of them in Zion appeareth before God." Zion is the place where man meets with God. Zion is the reality of the rent veil. As another Psalmist puts it in Psalm 87:5: "Of Zion it shall be said, This and that man was born in her.." Zion is the birthplace of saviours! "And saviours [or deliverers] shall come up on mount Zion..." (Obad.1:21). *Deliverance* is what David's Tabernacle is all about. Those who catch the vision of Zion are those who desire to bring salvation and *deliverance* to the nations. I believe with all of my heart that this is the heart cry of all who seek Him.

John the Baptist was being prepared for thirty years to fulfill *an 18-month ministry.* John's course was only eighteen months, but I would like to emphasize that he did fulfill his course! "And as John *fulfilled his course*, he said, Whom think ye that I am? I am not he..." (Acts 13:25). It is interesting that John was of the eighth course that David had ordained 1,000 years earlier.

The Lord Jesus Christ said on the final day of his three-and-a half year ministry: "I have *finished* the work which thou gavest me to do" (John 17:4).

The Apostle Paul declared in his final epistle: "I have *finished* my course, I have kept the faith.." (2 Tim. 4:7). Ten years earlier he told us the secret for fulfilling one's course in life. "But none of these things move me, neither count I my life dear unto myself, so that I might finish my course with joy, and the ministry which I have received of the Lord Jesus..." (Acts 20:24). If we want to finish our course and totally overcome the Adversary, we must not "love our life" or pamper ourselves (Rev.12:11).

The Scripture is filled with examples of people who made a very short debut upon the "holy stage." However, that *short debut* changed the course of human events. Like a star coming into its nova, they shined brilliantly for their time and season, fulfilling the purpose for which they were born. Esther means *"star"*. Her real destiny in this life only lasted a few days. We can only be perfect (complete) as we fulfill our course!

The porter courses

1 Chronicles 23:5 - "Moreover four thousand were porters..." Part of the Mount Zion organization was the appointment of the porter courses. These men too were divinely appointed, and they were all Levites. The porter is the *doorkeeper.* He is the one who carefully guards the door and only admits those who are of the "fold." The man who fills this position is faithful and responsible. As Jesus said Himself: "To him the porter openeth" (John 10:3).

The porters not only kept the gates of the city, but they kept the doors of David's house (the Church). They kept the temple gates and the doors of the treasuries, etc. Even in the future temple of Ezekiel, we find that there are six guard stations at each entry (Eze. 40:21 Amp.). The porter can speak of the faithful minister who keeps the door of his fold. He guards against the infiltration of those who would seek to destroy the work. "...And commanded the porter to watch" (Mark 13:34).

It is also interesting that these courses of porters kept the city gates twenty-four hours a day. Do you see who is supposed to be guarding the doors of their city? The ministers! Revivals bring about the unanimity of the ministers to "watch in prayer" for their city.

The doorkeeper

David's Tabernacle represents the true Church order. Thus, we must realize the importance of the position of the literal doorkeeper. It is said that the *first impression* is the one that lasts. When someone comes to visit our church, what kind of a reception do they receive? We once visited a church that had a husband and wife team at each door. They had courses in this church. There was such a sense of security and hospitality displayed there. We had with us a man who was not walking with the Lord, but he was greatly impressed with the reception. Never underestimate this position!

The Psalmist said: "I had rather be a doorkeeper in the house of my God, than to dwell in the tents of wickedness" (Psa. 84:10). In essence he was saying that the pleasure experienced standing at the threshold of the Lord's house was better than all the pleasures that sin affords!

Other appointments of David

David's Tabernacle substantiates the authority for every position in the Church, and the need for every part to function and supply. Paul uses the word "governments" (administrative positions). He also uses the word "helps." Helps can cover a wide variety of skills that not every one can supply, Such as the cook. (See 1 Cor.12:28, Eph 4:16.) Every part of the body of Christ is needed in order to supply for the whole. A lady once told us that the Lord gave her the verse: "Feed my sheep." She took that verse very literally and became the camp cook. She was very appreciated, I might add!

The Deacon board is not just a status position or some elected position. Deacons also are appointed from above, and that is New Testament theology. Acts 6:3-6 - The deacon board basically administrates the menial business of the local church. (See 1 Chr. 26:29-30.)

Treasurers (1 Chr. 9:26, 26:26-28) David appointed treasurers. His treasury entailed a lot of work. When revival comes there will be a tremendous amount of money flowing in and out of the church, and this is when we will come to appreciate a good steward.

The Recorder (1 Chr. 16:4) was the "secretary." He kept all of the records and the history, etc. This position is very important, especially in a church that publishes the gospel on the page. Throughout Zion fellowship, we have many that handle the pen. To have those with secretarial skills is an immense blessing! (Judges 5:14) - "… and out of Zebulun they that handle the pen of the writer." Anointed scribes recorded much of the Scripture.

The Food Bank (1 Chr. 28:25-29) David even had his appointments over the food store. Part of the responsibility of the church is to minister to the poor. In fact, that is what the early deacons did in Acts chapter 6. People who serve in these capacities are actually freeing up the ministry to perform their divine tasks, and thus will partake with them in the eternal rewards.

The Nethinims (Ezra 8:20) "Also of the Nethinims, whom David and the princes had appointed for the service of the Levites." Here is a group appointed by David that you don't hear much about. This group was assigned to the most menial of all tasks. They had to carry wood or water. Perhaps they had to clean the animal waste from the courts or scrub the utensils. They were the *custodians* of God's house. I depend very much upon the services of my custodian. I wish more people would be willing to begin here!

What is rather interesting about this group is that they were some of the very first to return from the Babylonian captivity. They were assigned to be quartered in the water gate section of the city. That might not mean too much, except for the fact that this is where the revival began during the Feast of Tabernacles. For the water gate revival, see Nehemiah chapter 8.

CHAPTER TEN

Zion's Standard

Another prominent aspect of Mount Zion is its *standard.* As we are about to learn in this chapter, the measuring stone is laid in Zion, and that stone is *Christ!* In the end, anything that does not meet the true standard of Christ shall not have a part in this glorious building—the glorious Church.

The Cornerstone of Zion

Isaiah 28:16-17 "Therefore thus saith the Lord GOD, Behold, *I lay in Zion* for a foundation a stone, a tried stone, a precious corner stone, a sure foundation: he that believeth shall not make haste. Judgment also will I lay to the line, and righteousness to the plummet: and the hail shall sweep away the refuge of lies, and the waters shall overflow the hiding place."

The cornerstone is the most important stone in the building because all the other stones must square to it. Isaiah said there is a line stretched horizontally, and a plumb dropped vertically to this stone. Every part of the building is judged by the precept of this "stone." Isaiah goes on to tell us, that anything that does not measure to this *stone in Zion* shall be swept away by the storm. Anything that does not agree with this stone is a falsehood. We can see in these few verses why there is a storm of "great tribulation" coming to the latter house. This storm will test the doctrines of men, and everything that can be shaken will be shaken so that only that which is true might remain!

This certainly agrees with the doctrine of Christ. Matthew 7:24-27 states: "Therefore whosoever heareth these sayings of mine, and doeth them, I will liken him unto a wise man, which built his house upon a rock: And the rain descended, and the floods came, and the winds blew, and beat upon that house; and it fell not: for it was founded upon a rock. And every one that heareth these sayings of mine, and doeth them not, shall be likened unto a foolish man, which built his house upon the sand: And the rain descended, and the floods came, and the winds blew, and beat upon that house; and it fell: and great was the fall of it." (See also Hebrews 12:26-28.)

Peter defines this Stone laid in Zion as the Lord Jesus Christ (1 Pet. 2:6-8). This is why Zion speaks of the high standard. Those who come up to Zion are qualified by squaring up to the doctrine of Christ. Zion represents the *"tried stones."* After all, Zion is where the government emerges.

* Note: To the disobedient this stone is also called *the stumbling stone.* Even in Zion God allows His doctrine to trip up the hypocrite. 1 Peter 2:8 - "a stone of stumbling, and a rock of offence, even to them which stumble at the word, being disobedient: whereunto also they were appointed."

Being measured in the Upper Room

On the eve of the crucifixion Christ brought His disciples up to Mount Zion to a room where they would keep the Passover. Most people do not realize where this room was located because it is not recorded in Scripture. The "upper room" is a historical place upon the ancient Mount Zion. Though these twelve men did not realize what was transpiring that night, they were being *measured.* They were being washed by the water of the Word. Christ as "the laver" was giving them a reflection of themselves in a way they could only understand afterward.

"What I do thou knowest not now; but thou shalt know hereafter" (John 13:7).

While the disciples were arguing over who would be the greatest, they were but a few hours away from being scattered like sheep. What a revelation they were about to have of themselves that night, of their motives, rivalry, indifference, unbelief, and contradiction! Coming to Zion means that God is going to quite expose our hearts, but that is good because he that comes to the light wants to be cleansed by that light! (See John 3:21.)

The law from Zion

"For out of Zion shall go forth the law, and the word of the LORD from Jerusalem" (Isa. 2:3). Notice the contrast between "the word of the Lord" and "the law of the Lord." Zion is higher than Jerusalem. The law goes forth from Zion, which speaks of the higher position, and the word of the Lord goes forth from Jerusalem. The law can tend to offend Christians because it deals with the old nature. Of course, that is what this veil-less tent is all about—people who have had their old nature crucified.

King David declared in Psalm 19:7: "The law of the LORD is perfect, converting the soul." In this Psalm, David compares the precision of the universe to God's law. The heavens declare His awesome measure and accuracy. Every celestial body is in its circuit, fulfilling its course. Those who measure time and space can attest to the accuracy of the stars. The Naval Observatory in Washington adjusts our national clock to a particular star in the heavens.

God's law does not contain errors, and His judgments are infallible. Jesus made this comment concerning the law in Matthew 5:18: "For verily I say unto you, Till heaven and earth pass, one jot or one tittle shall in no wise pass from the law, till all be fulfilled." A jot or tittle is equivalent to a dot of an i or the crossing of a t. Christ also stated that those who uphold the law and teach it shall be called "great in the kingdom" (Mt. 5:19). Jesus came to fulfill the law in truth and in deed, and He taught that love fulfills the law in truth and deed. (Also see Rom. 13:9-10.)

The law offends the flesh

Most Christians are not offended by the Word of the Lord. Stories of faith, the message of redemption, the message of healing, miracles, provision, compassion, mercy, and love do not offend God's people. However, it is the message of the cross that is offensive to God's people. It is not offensive that *Christ* died on a cross, but the idea that *we* must bring our old nature to the cross and die to self is offensive! This is the message that offends man.

The New Covenant is the fulfilling of the law. It can never happen unless we die to self. As the Apostle Paul declares: "That the righteousness of the law might be fulfilled in us, who walk not after the flesh, but after the Spirit. For if ye live after the flesh, ye shall die: but if ye through the Spirit do mortify the deeds of the body, ye shall live" (Rom. 8:4, 13). We can only fulfill the law as we walk in the Spirit, and we can only walk in the Spirit as we crucify the flesh with its affections. (See also Galatians 5:16-24.)

Compromise restricts the ministry to the outer court

Many churches are very careful not to uphold too high a standard because they are afraid it will reduce the size of their congregation. I once had a pastor tell me that he had about a dozen marriages coming up that summer. He also went on to tell me that they were all second or third time marriages. Then he looked at me rather sheepishly and said, "Well, we have got to keep them in the Church, you know!"

Ministers often compromise God's standard just to have a larger church. In fact, that is the reason that many of the Old Testament priests were sentenced to remain in the outer court (Ezk. 44:10-14). They allowed the people to bring their idols into the hallowed place. "Because they ministered unto them before their idols."

We have seen churches compromise their worship services and allow "Christian rock" so that they could keep the young people. May I say that when God's standard is compromised, another spirit comes in! Having a big congregation should never be the primary objective of the pastor. The top priority should be to lead the flock into the paths of righteousness and truth!

Someone was telling us about a pastors' seminar they attended where the main emphasis was on church growth. One of the *words of caution* mentioned in this seminar was that the pastor should never mention the word "holiness." In other words, the thought of holiness or having a standard would keep people from coming to church. Yet, Zion is actually called the mountain of His holiness (Obad.1:17, Psa. 48:1).

A popular radio teacher once said that if we wanted to have a big church the sermon should never go over fifteen or twenty minutes. Sad as it is, this is too often the way it is in the Church world today. Many Christians do not want anything that demands study or concentration, or anything that is too convicting.

Truth is divisive

"I came not to send peace, but a sword" (Mt.10:34, cf. Lk.12:51-53). Although the seminar lecturer warned the pastors never to speak on divisive issues, he forgot to tell them the disservice they are doing their flock, for they are depriving them of ever ascending into the high places of God.

Psalm 15:1-2 - "LORD, who shall abide in thy tabernacle? who shall dwell in thy holy hill? He that walketh uprightly, and worketh righteousness, and speaketh the truth in his heart." When I was a young Christian, my heart cry was for truth. The thoughts of milling around the shadowy valleys of confusion were intolerable to me. I really am not afraid to follow a leader if I believe he knows where he is going, but I get a little nervous if he can never give any clear answers.

Jesus made it quite plain that He did not come to bring peace, but division. The sword of truth separates those who want to follow Him. Yes, we can enjoy the peace of complacency or the peace of apathy, or the peace of ignorance and indifference; but it is not the true peace (See Mt.10:34-42).

Paul told his converts right up front that the way into the kingdom was "through much tribulation" (Acts 14:22). That did not offend them! It is more offensive to say: "Come to Jesus and your troubles will be over," only to be *disillusioned* later when trouble comes.

The Scriptures exhort us to "buy the truth and sell it not" (Pro. 23:23). This indicates there is a price to pay for truth. The Laodiceans were told to buy…. The five foolish virgins were also told to buy…. (See Mt. 25:9 and Rev. 3:18.) Zion not only represents the truth but those who *buy* the truth!

The Tabernacle of David—standard of righteousness and judgment

Isaiah 16:5 - "And in mercy shall the throne be established: and he shall sit upon it in truth *in the tabernacle of David,* judging, and seeking judgment, and hasting righteousness." The interesting thing about this verse is that it was penned about 300 years after David. This passage is an allusion to the Lord Jesus Christ's being enthroned in the Tabernacle of David and the fact that his throne would be the seat of righteousness, judgment, and mercy.

There is actually much to meditate upon in this verse. The fact that Christ wants to be enthroned in His Church puts us into the same scenario as when David wanted to bring the Ark back into the midst of his people. We often sing choruses proclaiming Jesus as Lord or enthroning Him with our songs, but He really does not reign unless certain criterion has been meet. A church can actually limit the reigning capacity of Christ. Psalm 78:41 proves this: "Yea, they turned back and tempted God, and *limited* the Holy One of Israel." Man was created with the power of choice, and although Christ has all power to do whatever He wishes, He allows His people to limit what He does. If a church does not believe in healing and will not proclaim Him as healer, do not expect to be healed there.

Christ wants to be enthroned in such a way that His Church reflects and enacts His righteous judgments. The Apostle Paul said that the Church is to be "the pillar and ground of truth" [the guiding pillar, the foundation of truth.] (1 Tim. 3:15). How can a Church that compromises God's law and standard expect the Lord to be seated there, hasting righteousness and judgment?

God's standard of righteousness

All of the redeemed are declared to be *righteous* by virtue of the blood of Jesus. This is called "imputed righteousness." However, there is another form of the word which means "imparted righteousness." That Greek word is *dikaioma* which means "righteous works." This particular word is found in Revelation 19:8: "And to her was granted that she should be arrayed in fine linen, clean and white: for the fine linen is the righteousness [righteous works] of saints." In your concordance it is #1345 - *dikaioma* (dik-ah'-yo-mah). This word is talking about the righteous *acts* of the saints. For example, the Bride is righteous because she *is* righteous! Not only has she been *counted* righteous, she has been *made* righteous. She reflects the righteousness of Christ in word and deed! This is the many-membered bridal company that reflects the image of the *Groom.* "Little children, let no man deceive you: he that *doeth* righteousness is righteous, even as he is righteous" (1 Jn. 3:7).

Psalm 15:1-2 - "Who shall abide in thy tabernacle? Who shall dwell in thy holy hill? He that walketh uprightly, *and worketh righteousness...*" God gives this gift of righteousness to those who are seeking after righteousness, even as Jesus taught upon the mount, "Seek ye first the kingdom of God, *and his righteousness...*" In that same sermon Jesus said: "Blessed are they that *hunger and thirst after righteousness,* for they shall be filled" (Mt. 5:6, 6:33).

The key for receiving the gift of righteousness is revealed in Psalm 24:3-6. Again we are told that they who are *seeking* after this gift shall receive it. "He shall receive the blessing from the LORD, and righteousness from the God of his salvation" (Psa. 24:5). Psalm 24 compares with Psalm 15. We will examine these Psalms later on in this study.

Please continue to bear in mind that David's

Tabernacle is a perfect representation of what the Lord Jesus Christ intended His Church to be!

The Church - a place of judgment

Isaiah 16:5 - "And he shall sit upon it in truth *in the tabernacle of David,* judging, and seeking judgment..." I once attended a pastor's seminar where a question and answer session was held at the conclusion of the meeting. One of the questions that was raised was, "Does the Church have the right to judge a person who has sinned?" The leaders of the seminar refused to answer the question.

One of the great misconceptions in the Church world is the idea that "We must not judge!" Certainly that has its application when balanced in the right setting, but a church that thinks they can sit by nonchalantly, trying to ignore all the existing sins, is truly a "Corinthian" church.

Jesus exhorted us to "judge righteous judgment" (Jn. 7:24). This indictment was against the hypocrites who passed sentence when they themselves were guilty. Paul said to the Corinthians: "Is there not a wise man among you who is able to judge between his brethren and make a sound judgment?" Then he reprimanded them for taking one another to court before the ungodly. (See 1 Cor. 6:5-6.) From these passages, we can see that the Church is to be a place of judgment!

The Corinthians execute judgment in the Church

The Apostle also exhorted this same Church to join in agreement together in judgment and to hand a blatant offender over to Satan to afflict him. (See 1 Cor. 5:1-5). This Church had tolerated a well-known act of unrepentant incest. The whole idea of this judgment was to bring about a repentance, which eventually did take place as we see in 2 Corinthians 2:6-7.

The Church - a place of mercy (Isaiah 16:5)

2 Corinthians 2:6-7 - "Sufficient to such a man is this punishment, which was inflicted of many. So that contrariwise ye ought rather to forgive him, and comfort him, lest perhaps such a one should be swallowed up with overmuch sorrow." Paul now exhorts the church to show mercy to the repentant man (Prov. 28:13). There can only be mercy when judgment has been satisfied. Mercy is shown only to those who are willing to confess and forsake their sins.

A great problem arises when leaders decide to pardon a serious offence when it is not in the mind of the Spirit. Pardon and forgiveness are two different things. David was immediately *forgiven* when he acknowledged his sin, but David was not *pardoned.* There were consequences. There were many judgments against his house before he was fully restored. If we pardon before God pardons, then the offender will offend again and perhaps even worse. "Let my sentence come forth from thy presence; let thine eyes behold the things that are equal" (Psa.17:2).

The Church is to be a place of judgment. Therefore, our sentence must come from heaven. The prophet Isaiah said that Jerusalem (a type of the Church) was once filled with judgment and righteousness, but that justice was now perverted there (cf. Isa.1:21). He goes on to tell of a purging that was coming, which would again reinstate them to be the faithful city (Isa.1:25-27).

Isaiah 1:21-22 - "How is the faithful city become an harlot! it was full of judgment; righteousness lodged in it; but now murderers. Thy silver is become dross, thy wine mixed with water."

Isaiah 1:25-27 - "And I will turn my hand upon thee, and purely purge away thy dross, and take away all thy tin: And I will restore thy judges as at the first, and thy counsellors as at the beginning: afterward thou shalt be called, The city of righteousness, the faithful city. Zion shall be redeemed with judgment, and her converts with righteousness."

* May I repeat that the Zadok priesthood was faithful to uphold the standard when the other priests were lax and let it down. The Zadokites were rewarded with special honor and God-given discernment. In controversial issues, they had the authority to stand. "And in controversy they shall stand in judgment; and they shall judge it according to my judgments: and they shall keep my laws and my statutes in all mine assemblies" (Eze. 44:24).

CHAPTER ELEVEN

Show Us the Way to Zion

Jeremiah 50:5 - "They shall ask the way to Zion." In this chapter we are going to take a little journey with the "pilgrim." The pilgrim is on his way to Mount Zion in a progressive series of psalms known as the "Pilgrim Psalms," or "The Song of Ascents."

The Lamb upon Mount Zion

Although we have used various *types* in this study, such as the manifest Ark upon Mount Zion, let us put all of that behind us for the moment and see the "Lamb" standing upon Mount Zion. This is what it is all about. Although Christ fills all things, yet He reserves an exclusive place to Himself upon the holy hill, and He seeks for those who are interested in the reality of knowing Him. So let everything fade from the background and see the *Lamb* standing upon Mount Zion: "And I looked, and, lo, a Lamb stood on the mount Sion" (Rev.14:1).

The journey

This journey begins with *a holy discontentment* of where we are dwelling spiritually. Because the Lord satisfies the desire and the longing of all who *seek Him,* it is as though a fresh vision is birthed within us. With that fresh vision comes a holy emulation and a resolve to press toward that end. Like the parable of the pearl of great price, the seeker is willing to sell all to gain all! "Again, the kingdom of heaven is like unto a merchant man, seeking goodly pearls: Who, when he had found one pearl of great price, went and sold all that he had, and bought it" (Mt.13:45-46).

The Pilgrim Songs

Toward the end of the Restoration Era, the Levite musicians put together a little Psalter that incorporated about fifteen psalms—Psalms 120-134.

As the pilgrims came up to "the holy city" to keep the three yearly feasts, they would sing these various psalms according to their proximity to the city. That is why these psalms are also called *"The Psalms of Degrees" or "Ascents."* The Hebrew word translated "degree" means "ascending higher."

The reason I am incorporating this series of songs into this study is because they reveal a *progression*. The pilgrims have a destination. They are slowly ascending to Zion, and it is in Zion that the blessing is bestowed! We will try to capture a little seed thought from each of these Psalms, just enough to establish the theme and also to encourage those who are still on this pilgrimage. You may find yourself on one of these plateaus.

PSALMS 120 –134

From the disunity and strife of the lower climb to the unity and blessing of Zion

Psalm 120

This series of Psalms begins with a heart cry for a better dwelling place in God: "Woe is me, that I sojourn in Mesech." (Vs. 5) Mesech, as presented in this Psalm, represents a place of discord and strife. The inhabitants are against everything that promotes harmony and unity. (Vs. 6) "My soul hath long dwelt with him that hateth peace." We will never leave our "Babylon" until we become very discontented!

Psalm 121

The sojourner now catches a vision for Zion: "I will lift up mine eyes to the hills." He is talking about the hills that encompass Zion (See Psa. 125:2). There was always a promise to the Israelite sojourner who was captive in a strange land, that if he would just turn his eyes and pray toward that city, God would hear!

2 Chronicles 6:38 - "If they return to thee with all their heart and with all their soul in the land of their captivity, whither they have carried them captives, and pray toward their land, which thou gavest unto their fathers, and toward the city which thou hast chosen, and toward the house which I have built for thy name..."

Psalm 122

The sojourner now has a great hunger for the presence of the Lord: "I was glad when they said unto me, Let us go into the house of the LORD." (Vs. 1) These Psalms all reflect the heart of God's people after they had returned from their exile. The purpose of the exile was to develop wholehearted-ness. Many times God's people take things for granted and thus become careless in their relationship. That is why God allows captivities to come, for they help us to refocus on the things that really matter.

Psalm 123

According to history, only one in ten caught the vision to return from their exile. Perhaps this is what Isaiah was alluding to in Isaiah 6:13: "But yet in it shall be a tenth, and it shall return." Unfortunately, there are too many Christians who are content to coexist with the world (worldly influences), and thus they succumb to mediocrity. The remnant that returned was greatly reproached: (Vs. 3-4) "Have mercy upon us, O LORD, have mercy upon us: for we are exceedingly filled with contempt. Our soul is exceedingly filled with the scorning of those that are at ease, and with the contempt of the proud."

With the vision comes a price to pay. Many times the greatest opposition to moving on in God is not from the world

but from within the ranks of the Church—
from those who are at ease. Reproach,
being rejected by his own Jewish brethren,
broke the heart of Christ.

Psalm 124

The pilgrim experiences divine help: "If it
had not been the LORD who was on our
side, when men rose up against us: Then
they had swallowed us up quick, when their
wrath was kindled against us" (Psa.
124:2,3). This Psalm in a sense follows the
same plight as the previous Psalm, except
now the opposition is from the world. The
world fights against the pilgrim, and the
world tries to kill the pilgrim, as in the
"Vanity Fair" mentioned in John Bunyan's
book entitled *Pilgrim's Progress.* However,
the Lord is on our side! Amen!

Psalm 125
(Faith keeps us upon this road.)

The Psalmist declares that there shall
be a sifting along this road, (See vs. 5.)
but: "They that trust in the LORD shall be
as mount Zion, which cannot be removed,
but abideth for ever." God allows many
things to test the faith of His pilgrims

along this journey, but those who trust in the Lord shall be as Mount Zion. Mount Zion symbolizes an abiding place in Christ that is *unshakable.* The Church in its truest sense cannot be shaken!

Psalm 46:5 - "God is in the midst of her; she shall not be moved: God shall help her, and that right early." (See also Psalms 46, 47, 48.)

Psalm 126

This Psalm begins on a high note: "When the LORD turned again the captivity of Zion, we were like them that dream. Then was our mouth filled with laughter, and our tongue with singing." The release from captivity, the vision, and the renewed exuberance is finally tempered with the grim reality. As the exiles return with their hearts burning with the message of restoration, they are suddenly confronted with a city in ruins. The Psalmist continues: "They that sow in tears shall reap in joy" (Vs. 5). There can never be a return without an investment! There is a cost involved when we are traveling to Zion, but in the end the dividends far outweigh the cost!

Psalm 127

"Except the LORD build the house, they labour in vain that build it: except the LORD keep the city, the watchman waketh but in vain." One of the most important lessons that we learn along this highway to Zion is the lesson of *true grace.* We can only walk this highway by grace! We can do all the right things and fail! We can live by all the principles, but if our trust is in some spiritual equation, we will fail. There are times in this spiritual walk when we are challenged by the Spirit to do something that does not jive with our *book of principles,* even though the principle in itself is right. We have known people who have tried to save their home and family by not moving on with God, but in the end their house crumbled! They were obeying *concepts* over the Holy Spirit's conviction.

Psalm 128

If we walk with the Lord, we will have many spiritual children, and our offspring will resemble us. The Lord desires us to bring forth a holy seed. (See Mal. 2:15.) One of the blessings of this plateau is this:

"Thou shalt see thy children's children, and peace upon Israel" (Vs. 6.) I think one of the greatest encouragements in this life is to see our natural and spiritual children seeking after righteousness!

Psalm 129

In reflecting on the cruelty of the captivity, the Psalmist ends by saying that his captors did not prevail against him! "Many a time have they afflicted me from my youth: yet they have not prevailed against me" (Vs. 2) He further states that God had cut away the cords that bound him. Anyone who wants to progress onward will find himself in a prison of some kind. Joseph is an example of this. He went to prison for being righteous (Gen. 39:21). However, it is in this place of captivity that God gives us a heart to know him (See Jer. 24:5-7.) Every true son must be chastened. Chastening cleanses us from many inbred iniquities and propensities to sin, but when it is over it produces "the peaceable fruit of righteousness" (Heb.12:5-11).

Psalm 130

Psalm 130 continues with the thought of

being redeemed from all iniquity: "He shall redeem Israel from all his iniquities" (Vs. 8). Holiness is the standard for Mount Zion. As we study this Psalm, we see that Israel is reflecting upon the deep slough of sin and despair from which they had been rescued. Obviously, this had been the experience of the author of this Psalm, but it gives hope to all of us!

Psalm 131
Before honor is humility (cf. Prov.15:33, 18:12). "My heart is not haughty, nor mine eyes lofty" (Vs.1). One of the attributes of those who dwell upon Mount Zion in heaven is that they have the lamb-like nature of meekness and humility. People who have *submitted to the spiritual prisons* are such a people.

Psalm 132
"The LORD hath sworn in truth unto David; he will not turn from it; of the fruit of thy body will I set upon thy throne" (Vs.11). As the pilgrims sang this song, they were reminded that David's throne must continue. At this time in their history, David's throne had been discontinued.

They were also reminded that Zion was the eternal *rest* for God's people (Vs.13-14). I am sure that as they viewed Zion from a distance, their hopes were renewed.

For the Jews, the literal throne of David will not continue until the Millennial dispensation. Yet for the Church, we expect to see the full spiritual reality of this as Christ is enthroned in the Tabernacle of David in these last days. We will consider Zion's restoration later on in this study.

Psalm 133

The sojourner has finally reached his destination. He has ascended from the lower planes of unreality and discord, to the heights where he may enjoy the pleasantness of the people who are real and genuine. "Behold, how good and how pleasant it is for brethren to dwell together in unity!" Another beautiful aspect of the pilgrims who arrive here is that they are all of one spirit! Also notice that this unity is likened unto the anointing oil that was poured upon the High Priest. It is like the precious ointment upon the head, that ran down upon the beard, even Aaron's beard (Vs. 2). This is the anointing that allowed the High Priest to enter within the veil.

The anointing oil

The description of this anointing oil is found in Exodus 30:22-32.

Exodus 30:23-25 - "Take thou also unto thee principal spices, of *pure myrrh* five hundred shekels, and of *sweet cinnamon* half so much, even two hundred and fifty shekels, and of *sweet calamus* two hundred and fifty shekels, And of *cassia* five hundred shekels, after the shekel of the sanctuary, and of *oil olive* an hin: And thou shalt make it an oil of holy ointment, an ointment compound after the art of the apothecary: it shall be an holy anointing oil."

Shekel weight of the sanctuary:

500	pure myrrh	Myrrh speaks of *meekness, or death to self.*
250	sweet cinnamon	Cinnamon speaks of *goodness.*
250	sweet calamus	Calamus speaks of *gentleness.*
500	cassia	Cassia speaks of *humility.*

The constituency of unity

Where all of these spiritual spices exist, there cannot be anything but unity! Also notice that the weight of these spices tally up to 1500 which speaks of the law. 1500 is the dimension of the outer court, which represents the age of the law. Therefore, those who have come to Zion have fulfilled the law, and that is the reality of the New Covenant!

*Note: Olive oil speaks of peace, and all of these virtues produce peace. These virtues do not come without a great personal cost of suffering. It take the "oil press" to produce the oil. *Gethsemane* means "the oil press."

Psalm 133:3 - "As the dew of Hermon, and as the dew that descended upon the mountains of Zion: *for there the LORD commanded the blessing, even life for evermore."* This is what this whole study is about—coming to Mount Zion. Herein is life abundant! "I am come that they might have life, and that they might have it more abundantly" (John 10:10).

Psalm 134

This final Psalm is a doxology. As the pilgrims prepared to return to their respective places, the priests would proclaim the blessings of Zion upon them: "The LORD that made heaven and earth bless thee out of Zion." Now they can return to bless and be a blessing! Amen. We will consider the blessings of Zion more specifically later on.

This series of Psalms has taken us taken us through a number of experiences that every pilgrim must face. The lessons we learn as we walk in the Spirit are the lessons that will qualify us to partake of the high calling.

CHAPTER TWELVE

The Qualifications for Zion

As we have stated during various intervals of this book, there are qualifications that must be met in order to know the full blessing of this holy mountain. We do not arrive here by being born again, but it is reserved for those "who follow on to know Him." In this chapter we are going to consider the qualifications that are necessary to *"come up hither."* Psalms 15 and Psalm 24 will be the central focus of this chapter.

The question

In Psalm fifteen, David asks the question: "Lord,

who shall abide in thy tabernacle? Who shall dwell in thy holy hill?" This Psalm is penned after David has planted the tabernacle upon Mount Zion, and is awestruck by this new plateau upon which he finds himself. He realizes that one cannot just walk up to this place any more than one can walk into the Holy of Holies. It is here that David receives the inspiration for this Psalm.

Psalm fifteen

15:1
"LORD, who shall abide in thy tabernacle? who shall dwell in thy holy hill?"

15:2
"He that walketh uprightly, and worketh righteousness, and speaketh the truth in his heart."

15:3
"He that backbiteth not with his tongue, nor doeth evil to his neighbour, nor taketh up a reproach against his neighbour."

15:4
"In whose eyes a vile person is contemned; but he honoureth them that

fear the LORD. He that sweareth to his own hurt, and changeth not."

15:5
"He that putteth not out his money to usury, nor taketh reward against the innocent. He that doeth these things shall never be moved."

Eleven qualifications

In answer to the question that David asks in the first verse ("Who shall dwell in thy holy hill?"), there are eleven qualifications given in the following verses. Let us briefly examine them:

He who walketh uprightly

The word "upright" in Hebrew has the sense of walking perfectly. God told Abraham to walk before him and be perfect (Gen.17:1). We may ask, "How is that possible?" *It is possible* to be perfect as we walk in the light (or in the truth) that God has revealed. The Apostle John said that if we walked in the light, the blood of Christ would continually cleanse us. (See 1 John 1:7.) We can be perfect as we walk in obedience to the revealed truth.

Worketh righteousness

As you will recall from an earlier part of this study, there is a difference between the passive righteousness and the outworked righteousness. We are declared righteous at salvation by doing nothing *except believing.* However, those in the "bridal company" are righteous because they are righteous in deeds and truth. It is a part of their clothing!

Speaketh the truth in his heart

Our conference president put it very well when he said: "Our heart agrees with our mouth." David himself said: "Behold, thou desirest truth in the inward parts" (Psa. 51:6).

Backbiteth not

The Hebrew word for backbite is "to slander or to defame." Many try to exalt themselves by defaming others, but they will not be exalted to the holy hill. The picture that we see in Revelation 14:5 is a group of followers who *"have no guile in their mouth."*

Nor doeth evil to his neighbor

Most Christians would never see themselves as

one that would purposely do evil to his neighbor. However, if you examine this thought in light of what Jesus taught about the Good Samaritan, the Levite who passed by the wounded and bleeding man was guilty of doing evil to his neighbour by doing nothing. (See Luke 10:29-37.)

Nor taketh up a reproach against his neighbour

Psalm one especially condemns those who sit on the scorner's bench. Those who mock, ridicule, or disdain their neighbor have no promise of blessing. Jesus Himself said that it was a serious offence to call your brother "worthless" (or "Raca" cf. Mt. 5:22).

Contemns those who are vile

This person despises those who practice evil. He will not recognize them or honor them. I think a good example of this would be Mordecai: " And all the king's servants, that were in the king's gate, bowed, and reverenced Haman: for the king had so commanded concerning him. But Mordecai bowed not, nor did him reverence" (Est. 3:2).

But he honors those who fear the Lord

The Lord said, "I will honor those who honor

me" (1 Sam. 2:30). We want to honor those whom the Lord honors. (See also Psalm 119:63.)

He that sweareth to his own hurt and changeth not (Vows)

This is a person who has made an agreement or a vow and then realizes that he will come up short, but he keeps that vow anyway. God is very cognizant of such agreements. We live in a society today that is very slack in honoring their commitments, especially in the area of marriage vows. Even in the Church, the divorce rate is not far behind the world, a fact that clearly tells the world that we have no more power than they do! This is a reproach to Christ.

That putteth not out his money to "usury" (Interest)

According to the law, one could not lend out his money for interest *to his brethren.* However, he could lend out his money for interest *to the world.* Deuteronomy 23:19-20 confirms this. There is also a wonderful promise to those who lend interest-free to their brethren. They shall be blessed in all that they put their hand to!

"Thou shalt not lend upon usury to thy brother; usury of money, usury of victuals, usury of any thing that is lent upon usury: Unto a stranger thou mayest lend upon usury; but unto thy brother thou shalt not lend upon usury: that the Lord thy God may bless thee in all that thou settest thine hand to in the land whither thou goest to possess it" (Deut. 23:19-20).

Nor taketh a reward against the innocent (a bribe)

Many of us would not consider ourselves guilty of receiving bribes per sé. However, there are a lot of situations in which people commit this infraction in a more subtle manner. Consider the case in a church where an offending party is a part of a large family. In order to vindicate the innocent, the pastor or elders would have to step on a lot of toes. Therefore, they evade the issue or decide to "let it heal itself." There are many incidents like this on secular jobs and in other areas of life. Showing favoritism and not executing justice in order to promote one's own advantage is another form of taking bribes.

These shall never be moved

Psalm fifteen ends with a promise that those who fulfill these qualifications *"shall never be moved."* This means that the qualifier shall be established upon the mount that shall never be moved. (See Psalm 125:1.)

Psalm Twenty-four

Psalm twenty-four has a theme similar to that of Psalm fifteen. The question is asked again concerning the privilege of ascending to the holy place upon Mount Zion: "Who shall ascend into the hill of the LORD? or who shall stand in his holy place?" (Psa. 24:3). In this Psalm, the qualifications are summarized into just four areas.

The four qualifications of Psalm 24

Psalm 24:4-5 - "He that hath clean hands, and a pure heart; who hath not lifted up his soul unto vanity, nor sworn deceitfully. He shall receive the blessing from the LORD, and righteousness from the God of his salvation."

Clean hands

David gives a good explanation for this term in Psalm 26:6: "I will wash mine hands in innocency: so will I compass thine altar, O LORD." "Clean hands," spiritually speaks of *innocence*. If you look at the context of this reference, David qualifies this by saying, "I will have no association with those who are contrary to God's way; I will not sit with them!" Simply put, we cannot have clean hands if we associate with the defiled!

A pure heart

Matthew 5:8 - "Blessed are the pure in heart: for they shall see God." Here is a prerequisite that tends to intimidate many, because impurity of heart is the most common plague of mankind. For one thing, we live in a society that promotes lust and promiscuity. Secondly, we live in *a "harvest generation."* What I mean by this is that this final generation inherits all the strengthening sins (and virtues) of the preceding generations. Often people suffer from lust and concupiscence simply because their progenitors never gained the victory in this area of their lives.

Even within the Church many suffer with spiritual maladies because the truth is obstructed. With every revelation of truth, however, comes a greater liberty. Christ fulfilled the five Levitical offerings (Leviticus 1-7), yet basically the Church only preaches one of them—the trespass offering. The trespass offering covers willful sins and sins of ignorance: "If we confess our sins, he is faithful and just to forgive us our sins, and to cleanse us from all unrighteousness" (1 Jn.1:9).

This is not having *dominion* over sin if we continually repeat the offence and continually ask forgiveness for the same offence. The "sin offering" is for the nature of sin. This does not mean that there is an eradication of the sin nature, but that there is victory over the nature of sin: "For sin shall not have dominion over you" (Rom. 6:14). Grace enables us to mortify or put to death our besetting sins, if we appropriate that grace.

I think that we should all take hope, realizing that even in the inner circle of Christ there were those who had been plagued with very demonic problems. Mary of Magdala was very close to the Lord Jesus. She had been possessed with seven evil spirits but was now clean. David said in Psalm 51:10, "Create in me a clean heart, O God." Being born again is like physical birth—the circumcision comes after we are born.

Nor lifted up his soul unto vanity

The word "vanity" (as used here) speaks of *idolatry or deceptive allusion.* From the New Testament perspective, the apostle Paul equates idolatry with covetousness (cf. Col. 3:5). Covetousness is an excessive love for anything. All things can be legitimate if they are kept in their proper focus or balance—a career, education, home, family, relationships, entertainment, etc. These things become idolatrous when they begin to displace our relationship with God the Father and the Lord Jesus Christ. The Apostle John said that the world is antichrist, and "if we love the world, the love of the Father is not in us." (See 1 John 2:15.)

Nor sworn deceitfully

Again we are coming back to the thought of taking an oath or a vow. The company that ascends Mount Zion is a group that *keeps their word* (cf. Rev.14:1-5). Psalm 24:4 is similar to the verse we looked at in Psalm 15:4. In the above passage, to "swear deceitfully" is to take a vow with no intention of honoring it! However, in Psalm 15:4, the vow is taken in good faith and is honored in spite of the consequences: "He that sweareth to his own hurt, and changeth not." It says of the group in heaven: "And in their mouth was found no guile" (Rev.14:5).

He shall receive the blessing

"He shall receive the blessing from the LORD, and righteousness from the God of his salvation" (Psa. 24:5). Here are the rewards of those who have qualified to ascend the holy hill: These receive "the blessing from the Lord" and the gift of righteousness. The gift of righteousness is different from the righteousness we receive at salvation. The righteousness mentioned here is *imparted* righteousness. It requires imparted righteousness to reign with Christ (cf. Rom. 5:17). Those who reign in the Millennium must qualify: "Blessed and holy is he that hath part in the first resurrection: on such the second death hath no power, but they shall be priests of God and of Christ, and shall reign with him a thousand years" (Rev. 20:6).

To qualify a people

The ministry of John the Baptist was to prepare a people for the *first* coming of Christ. Much more does this ministry need to be realized today—to prepare a people for the *Second Coming* of Christ, and to show them the way.

> *"To make ready a people prepared for the Lord."*
>
> *Luke 1:17*

CHAPTER THIRTEEN

Zion's Blessing

The past chapter concluded with the thought, *"He shall receive the blessing."* We have examined many of the factors that qualify us to ascend to this holy position, but now we will contemplate *the benefits* that make this pilgrimage well worth the effort.

Zion, Church of the firstborn

Hebrews 12:22-23 - "But ye are come unto mount Sion, and unto the city of the living God, the heavenly Jerusalem ... to the general assembly and church of the firstborn, which are written in heaven..." It is interesting that the Church upon Zion is called "the Church of the firstborn." That certainly draws a distinction within the Church body.

The firstborn always had the dominance and privilege over the other sons. Below is a list of a few of the rights given to firstborns:

- The firstborn expressed the strength, dignity, and excellence of power of his progenitor (Gn.49:3).
- The firstborn belonged to the Lord (Ex. 22:29).
- The firstborn was later represented by the ministry (Num. 8:18).
- The firstborn received the double portion (Deut. 21:17).
- The firstborn basically had the family mantle and was the spiritual head of his brethren.

Christ the Firstborn

The word *firstborn* in the Greek basically means "prototype" (Gr. prototokos). The first begotten reflects the father's image. Christ is called the first-born among many brethren. In other words, Christ was the firstfruit or sample of what God the Father desires: "For whom he did foreknow, he also did predestinate to be conformed to the image of his Son, that he might be the *firstborn* among many brethren" (Rom. 8:29).

The purpose of God is to bring many sons to glory (cf. Heb. 2:10). There will be a group that ascends higher than the others and they are changed as they behold him. The Apostle John tells us of such a group that emerges out from "the woman" (the woman is the Church), and this group is caught up into heavenly places to reign with Christ: "And she brought forth a manchild who was to rule all nations with a rod of iron" (Rev.12:1-5). This "manchild" is interpreted to mean, *a mature son.* "For as many as are led by the Spirit of God, they are the sons of God" (Rom. 8:14). The mature sons have come up the holy hill and have experienced the reality of David's Tabernacle, the New Covenant.

If we examine our originating chapter (Hebrews 12:5-17), we find quite a message on "true sonship." The true son receives chastening and will accept correction. In that same chapter we also read about another firstborn son named Esau who was profane and was rejected from inheriting his birthright blessing: "Lest there be any fornicator, or profane person, *as Esau,* who for one morsel of meat sold his birthright. For ye know how that afterward, when he would have inherited the blessing, he was rejected: for he found no place of repentance, though he sought it carefully with tears" (12:16,17).

The Hebrew word for *blessing* (berakah) is

virtually an anagram of the word that means both *birthright* and *firstborn* (bekorah).

Many Forfeit the Blessing

It is interesting that in the Millennium, Mount Zion has dominion over the Mount of Esau. Esau represents those who have forfeited their inheritance: "And saviours shall come up on mount Zion to judge the mount of Esau; and the kingdom shall be the LORD'S" (Obad.1:21). We are warned many times to guard our crown, and to guard against losing the reward that we have gained! (See 11 John 8, Rev. 3:12.) The high calling of the Church is to heavenly Zion, and for those who ascend, the "first-born blessing" is theirs!

Many of the people on earthly Mount Zion in David's time were *Levites.* This tribe was given *the right of the firstborn* when the other tribes of Israel forfeited that privilege. See the following Scriptures: 1 Chron.16:1, 4-6; Num. 3:12, 41, 45.

The blessing of Zion's roll call

One of the great blessings in eternity will take place during the "graduation day exercises." There has to be a royal occasion in heaven where some receive the crown, or the "eternal name," the merits, distinctions, or rewards. All of Scripture alludes to such an event!

Therefore, let us come back to our opening verses: "And church of the firstborn, which are written in heaven" (Heb.12:23). Although all of God's people are written in the Lamb's Book of life, there shall be special recognition to those who have appropriated Zion's call. I would suggest that this is what the Psalmist is referring to in Psalm 87:5-6: "And of Zion it shall be said, This and that man was born in her: and the highest himself shall establish her. The LORD shall count, when he writeth up the people, that this man was born there."

The Zion roll call in heaven is saying in effect that these are the firstborn, and all of the firstborn privileges belong to them. In heaven there are many echelons and ruling positions. There will be those who will be recognized, and there will be those who are not. (See Matthew 5:19.)

The blessing

Before we actually consider these blessings, I think we should understand something about the importance of "the blessing." In my former ignorance, I was not interested in the blessing per se`. I think that was mainly because of how I was led by some people to define it—a euphoric feeling, some monetary or material enrichment, etc. I hated to think of myself as a follower of Christ just for the loaves and the fishes.

I have come to find out that although God's blessing can be quite tangible, the real blessing is *a spiritual endowment* without which we cannot reign. Without this endowment we cannot be a blessing to God's people or to God Himself. Those who reign in the Millennium have obtained this *blessing.* To make it into the Millennium, one must be "blessed and holy" (Rev. 20:6). The word <u>*blessed*</u> means, "supremely blessed!" Jacob saw more than materialism in the blessing (Gen. 32:26). Elisha was so interested in that double portion that he thought it was worth pursuing Elijah relentlessly until he received it. We *must* have it! Amen!

Joseph's life illustrates the blessing

Joseph's life fulfills all of the types when it comes to the blessing. Such will be the case of all of those who receive the blessing. Joseph was tested and had to qualify before he inherited the promise. When Joseph was just a teenager he had dreams of his brethren, and even his parents bowing to him (bowing, not in the sense of worship, but bowing in respect for his position.) Joseph's mother never lived to see what became of Joseph, so there must be an eternal fulfillment here. These are all eternal truths: "Hear the word of the LORD, ye that tremble at his word; Your brethren that hated you, that cast you out for my name's sake, said, Let the LORD be glorified: but he shall appear to your joy, and they shall be ashamed" (Isa. 66:5).

Joseph demonstrated through his life and ministry what the Church upon Mount Zion shall do. The nations came to him for bread and for provision. Joseph had power to bless and he had power to bind princes and to teach wisdom. (See Psalm 105:21-22.) The real ministry is reserved for the spiritual firstborn. Jesus said that the Church would do even greater works than He had done. (See John 14:12). Even that statement shows the tremendous humility of Christ, that He would allow those inferior to Him to do greater miracles than He did. The Church has yet to enter into the full reality of this, but they shall.

Joseph's name was very great. Not only did his brethren have to bow the knee, but the world had to bow before Joseph also (See Gen. 41:40-44). One of the promises to those who have paid the price of separation was that they will have an eternal name: " I will make thy name to be remembered in all generations: therefore shall the people praise thee forever and ever" (Psa. 45:17).

Many ranks in eternity

- Some have an eternal name. (Psalm 45:17)
- Some sit with Christ in his throne. (Revelation 3:21)
- Some have crowns. (11 Timothy 4:7-8)
- Some are called great. (Matthew 5:19)
- The reverse of this is also true, for some are called *"the least in the kingdom."*

We are talking about the firstborn blessing, and yet Joseph was the eleventh son of Jacob. That tells us that election still ruled, even in the Old Testament. The first ten brothers were disqualified from the blessing. It is also interesting that when Jacob pronounced the birthright blessing upon Joseph, he is invoking a compound blessing: "The blessings of thy father have prevailed above the blessings of my progenitors unto the utmost bound of the everlasting hills: they shall be on the head of Joseph, and on the crown of the head of him that was separate from his brethren" (Gen. 49:26).

The double portion

Joseph received the double portion. In fact, two tribes emerge from Joseph. (See Gen. 48:9-20.) The double portion is for the Church of the Firstborn,

194

for it symbolizes the double inheritance, the double ministry, the double anointing. We will see later on that Zion must experience the atonement message, which means that God is cleansing Zion afresh. However, the Lord encourages His people that they shall have the double when the purging is over:

Isaiah 61:3-7 - "To appoint unto them that mourn in Zion, to give unto them beauty for ashes, the oil of joy for mourning, the garment of praise for the spirit of heaviness; that they might be called trees of righteousness, the planting of the LORD, that he might be glorified … For your shame *ye shall have double;* and for confusion they shall rejoice in their portion: therefore in their land *they shall possess the double:* everlasting joy shall be unto them."

"Ask of Me, and I shall give thee the heathen"
(Psalm 2:8)

The above verse is penned as David is sitting in the Tabernacle of Zion. David is challenged to ask for the nations. The emphasis in the Church world today seems to be more on evangelism than on character. Winning many people to Christ and having a large congregation seems to be the main focus. The paradox of the whole thing is that the people who have paid the price to have character; those who have been stripped and made barren by God (such as Joseph) will in the end claim far more people.

It is like the example Jesus gave to his disciples: "I sent you to reap that whereon ye bestowed no labour: other men laboured, and ye are entered into their labours" (Jn. 4:38). We know of a minister who was invited to preach in a certain Church in eastern Canada. While he was there revival broke out. His remarks about what happened came from John 4:38: "I sent you to reap where others have labored."

Perhaps the parable of the laborers in the vineyard would also be appropriate here. The eleventh hour workers were rewarded the same as those who had labored the whole day (cf. Mt. 20:1-16). The truth of this parable is simply that the eleventh hour workers were chosen! They are the people who have allowed God to deal with the issues in their lives. These have been willing to be deprived and have endured long seasons of barrenness. When the work is finished, they will accomplish more in six months than those who have labored for decades! (cf. Isa. 66:8).

Part of Joseph's blessing was the blessings of the womb, which means he was blessed with *many children*. Fruitfulness is the reward of those who fear the Lord. Notice this promise that was given to

Joseph: "Joseph is a fruitful bough, even a fruitful bough by a well; whose branches run over the wall" (Gen. 49:22). Essentially, this means that the blessing of God would extend to many people. Joseph's ministry touched many nations.

153 great fish (John 21:11)

The invitation to ask for the nations is given to those who have come up to Zion. The last miracle (or sign) that Jesus gave before His ascension was the catch of great fish. These fish were numbered and wherever there is a number in Scripture there is a revelation of truth. As you will recall from earlier in this study, 153 is the number of Zion (9 x 17 = 153). Nine speaks of fullness and seventeen speaks of spiritual perfection.

There is also another number mentioned in conjunction with this miracle: "For they were not far from land, but as it were two hundred cubits" (John 21:8). The number 200 is interpreted to mean, "the reward of the faithful." Jesus was showing his faithful servants what was about to take place. They were going to bring in a harvest of souls and the nets would hold the catch which were great fish. In Greek, the word translated "great" is *megas,* literally meaning *huge* fish—the kind all the fisherman dream of catching. (In your concordance it is # 3173 - megas)

It is one thing to have many little children, spiritually. It is quite another thing to have *full-grown* "sons." The great fish speak of those who will become the sons of God—those who will allow God to do something with their lives. The Apostle Paul raised up many fully-developed sons. John Wesley left behind 1100 ministers. The reward of the faithful is that they will reproduce many sons!

The overcomer

Mount Zion represents those who have overcome, and for them is the promise to inherit all things (Rev. 21:7). Those who win Christ in actuality win *everything!* He is their inheritance, and they are His inheritance among the people:

Revelation 2:26
"And he that overcometh, and keepeth my works unto the end, to him will I give power over the nations."

Revelation 2:27
"And he shall rule them with a rod of iron; as the vessels of a potter shall they be broken to shivers: even as I received of my Father."

Revelation 21:7

"He that overcometh shall inherit all things; and I will be his God, and he shall be my son."

Psalm 2:8

"Ask of me, and I shall give thee the heathen for thine inheritance, and the uttermost parts of the earth for thy possession. Thou shalt break them with a rod of iron; thou shalt dash them in pieces like a potter's vessel." This is a Mount Zion Psalm.

Zion, the final breakthrough

Although the greatest promises and blessing reside here, Zion was actually *the last place* to be inherited. The other tribes had entered their inheritance centuries before. Some had settled for an inheritance on the wilderness side of Jordan. Yet after David experienced his third anointing, he took the stronghold of Zion and then brought the Ark of the Covenant to rest upon that hill. It was here that the Lord said to David: "Ask of me, and I will give thee."

The Lord Bless Thee Out of Zion

Psalm 128:5
"The LORD shall bless thee out of Zion: and thou shalt see the good of Jerusalem all the days of thy life."

Psalm 132:15
"I will abundantly bless her provision: I will satisfy her poor with bread." (This is in reference to Zion.)

Psalm 133:3
"As the dew of Hermon, and as the dew that descended upon the mountains of Zion: for there the LORD commanded the blessing."

Psalm 134:3
"The LORD that made heaven and earth bless thee out of Zion."

CHAPTER FOURTEEN

The Redemption of Zion

Throughout this study we have magnified Zion's greatness, but now we have arrived at a chapter that needs some serious explanation. Why does Zion need to be redeemed? If she is so great and epitomizes those at the top, why then do we read passages that foretell of her refining? In this chapter we are going to consider why this purging is so necessary and what the outcome of this purging accomplishes. God is very jealous for His chosen one!

The foretelling of Zion's purge

Isaiah 1:27
"Zion shall be redeemed with judgement, and her converts with righteousness."

Isaiah 4:3
"And it shall come to pass, that he that is left in Zion, and he that remaineth in Jerusalem, shall be called holy, even every one that is written among the living in Jerusalem" (referring to a siege).

Isaiah 4:4
"When the Lord shall have washed away the filth of the daughters of Zion, and shall have purged the blood of Jerusalem from the midst thereof by the spirit of judgment, and by the spirit of burning."

Isaiah 10:12
"Wherefore it shall come to pass, that when the Lord hath performed his whole work upon mount Zion and on Jerusalem, I will punish the fruit of the stout heart of the king of Assyria, and the glory of his high looks" (referring to the judgment of Zion).

Isaiah 33:14

"The sinners in Zion are afraid; fearfulness hath surprised the hypocrites. Who among us shall dwell with the devouring fire? who among us shall dwell with everlasting burnings?"

These verses in Isaiah are telling us about a fiery siege that is coming against Zion to purge out the sinners and the hypocrites. Those who are purified through this trial shall be called holy, and Zion shall once again be renowned for its righteousness and judgment. The Assyrians happen to be the instrument being used to accomplish this judgment, but when they have accomplished their work on Zion, they are destroyed.

What has happened to Zion?

What has happened to Zion that would so kindle the wrath of the Lord's Spirit against them? The prophet himself said (in reference to Zion's behavior), that the Lord "looked for judgment but behold, oppression; for righteousness, but behold a cry" (a mournful cry).

It seems to be an unfortunate fact that revivals are short lived, and usually by the third generation the Church is in a serious declension. (See Judges

2:7-10.) Isaiah put it like this: "The people of thy holiness have possessed it but a little while…" (Isa. 63:18). I hope we are praying that this shall not be our case!

David only possessed Mount Zion for about ten years before his tragic fall. People often become careless after they have been in revival for a while. The Scripture bears out the fact that it is far more precarious to be in the place of great blessing than to be in a place of dire need (cf. Deut. 8:6-14).

David fell, and yet God did not let him remain in this pit. With great mercy and with great judgments, David was redeemed. At least fifteen judgments were levied against David, and they were heart-breaking judgments! Yet, David had a very glorious end! "And he died in a good old age, full of days, riches, and honour" (1 Chr. 29:28).

Not all are restored as David was because many Christians do not accept the punishments the way David did. Maybe they think they have suffered enough for their sin and begin to reject the very instrument that is doing the remedial surgery. We have known others who were flagrant offenders, yet God let them carry on undisciplined and uncorrected.

The Lord deals severely with His special ones

Often the Lord deals the hardest with those who

are going to reflect Him most. Every *son* must be "chastened" (Heb.12:6). Many who are in the Zion camp were *born* into it. These "children of Zion" are there by virtue of godly parents. Perhaps their parents have paid quite a price for the truth, and yet to the children, the truths of Zion are not experiential. They have not had to *buy* the truth! These truths must be bought.

I appreciated a comment that our conference president once made: He said that innocence is not the same as holiness. Innocence must be *tested* to become holiness. Children can be innocent when left in an environment that never challenges them.

The Lord does not want His people to ever remain in the "little children" state, but to progress on to "sonship." We must endure the trials and testing to become holy. The Apostle Paul tells of progressing on from righteousness unto holiness (Rom. 6:19).

The Lord is jealous for Zion

There are many reasons why Zion must be purified, but I think the main reason is because the Lord is *jealous* for Zion. "Thus saith the LORD of hosts; I was jealous for Zion with great jealousy, and I was jealous for her with great fury" (Zec. 8:2).

The Song of Songs presents a beautiful picture of God's special one. She had grown cold in her relationship. She had been so busy with her ministry in the vineyard that she had neglected the work in her own inner vineyard. After a series of dealings in her life, we see her emerging from the wilderness freshly endued with the glory of God. "Who is this that cometh up from the wilderness, leaning upon her beloved?" (See Song 1:6, 8:5.)

In the final chapter she says to her Lord: "Set me as a seal upon thine heart, as a seal upon thine arm: for love is strong as death; jealousy is cruel as the grave: the coals thereof are coals of fire, which hath a most vehement flame" (Song 8:6). What she is saying is, "Let the fire of thy jealousy be upon me." Be jealous for me ... "Don't let me go my own way or do my own thing!"

Job is another good case scenario. Job was tried to the extremity, while his friends went unscathed and untouched by the refining fires. However, in the end Job was on a far greater plane and he had the double portion.

The reasons for the fiery trial of Zion:

- To deal with the backsliders and those who had grown cold spiritually
- To remove the hypocrites and sinners (the chronic offenders)
- To prove those who had never been tested

- To bring His people into a greater degree of faith and blessing
- Ultimately, that Zion would be like that "tried stone" unto which all others measure

The siege of Zion

I would now like to devote several pages to the siege of Zion. We are looking at an event that took place during King Hezekiah's administration, in approximately 700 B. C. This siege encapsulates all that we have thus said in this chapter. It gives us a clear picture of why these things happen and what they accomplish. Lastly, it gives hope to those who may be going through similar spiritual experiences in their lives.

Revival precedes judgment

Hezekiah's reign began with a revival. This revival was one of the greatest in the Old Testament. Its impact was so great that it even penetrated into the Northern Kingdom which had already gone into captivity. Still, many from the north came down and experienced this great visitation of God. (See 2 Chronicles 29—31.)

This seems to be a principle that is substantiated throughout Scripture. The Lord *first* allows His people to experience His goodness, and His invitations of mercy and reconciliation. He allows them to see His power *before* He begins to deal seriously in their lives. The "Upper room" scene gives us a beautiful little picture of this. Jesus first allowed His disciples to taste His supper and to experience His goodness before He began to wash their feet.

Here are two major events—the revival, and the tribulation period that followed about fourteen years later. As we begin to contrast these two major events, we can see that there was more accomplished spiritually through the *siege* than from the revival.

God's people are not opposed to revivals, but when the revival ceases and the Lord begins to bring purifying trials into the camp, there is a lot of reaction! Yet these things are necessary to qualify or disqualify us for reigning with Christ. "And it shall come to pass, that he that is left in Zion, and he that remaineth in Jerusalem, shall be called holy, even every one that is written among the living in Jerusalem" (Isa. 4:3). The revival did not produce holiness, but the siege did!

The siege had been foretold

Isaiah 1:8 - "And the daughter of Zion is left as a cottage in a vineyard, as a lodge in a garden of cucumbers, as a besieged city." This siege did not come about by surprise. Zion saw this thing coming from a long way off. All of the surrounding nations had succumbed to the ravaging hordes of the Assyrians. Incidentally, the Assyrians are referred to as "the rod of God's anger." They were just *an instrument in the hand of the Lord.* "O Assyrian, the rod of mine anger, and the staff in their hand is mine indignation" (Isa.10:5). (See also 2 Samuel 7:14, and Psalm 17:13.)

Israel (the northern kingdom), had fallen over twenty years earlier, and now all of the cities of Judah had fallen. Basically, the old fortress of Zion was the last bastion within the kingdom, even as the prophet so poetically put it: "Till ye be left as a beacon upon the top of a mountain, and as an ensign on an hill" (Isa. 30:17).

They had plenty of time to make up their mind

What intensifies a trial is to see it coming from afar, slowly encroaching like a forest fire. You see the inevitability of the whole thing—like a creditor who is coming to collect, or like the specter of infirmity, etc.

Then to increase the tension further, the Assyrian herald would come and cry out to those who stood upon the city walls and tell them they were lame and powerless, and should give up (Isa. 36:1-20). Actually this whole scene foreshadows the last siege of Jerusalem and the Lord's intervention for His "Holy City." However, the point that I am trying to make here is that those who had taken refuge within the walls of Zion had time to decide whether they would submit to the siege or not!

Submit to the Lord - resist the siege

The word of the Lord to the inhabitants of Zion was to sit still and not to seek for help or counsel from anyone but the Lord Himself:

Isaiah 30:1
"Woe to the rebellious children, saith the LORD, that take counsel, but not of me; and that cover with a covering, but not of my spirit, that they may add sin to sin."

Isaiah 30:2
"That walk to go down into Egypt, and have not asked at my mouth; to strengthen themselves in the strength of Pharaoh, and to trust in the shadow of Egypt."

Isaiah 30:7
"For the Egyptians shall help in vain, and to

no purpose: therefore have I cried concerning this, Their strength is to sit still."

Isaiah 30:15
"For thus saith the Lord GOD, the Holy
One of Israel; In returning and rest shall
ye be saved; in quietness and in confidence shall be your strength: and ye would
not."

Isaiah 31:1
"Woe to them that go down to Egypt for
help; and stay on horses, and trust in chariots, because they are many; and in horsemen, because they are very strong; but
they look not unto the Holy One of Israel,
neither seek the LORD."

From these verses we can see exactly what was
happening—there was a mass exodus from the city.
They were fleeing to the refuge and covering of
Egypt, a type of the world. Even in spite of this,
Isaiah still urges them to return and to trust in the
Lord's redemption: "And ye would not, but ye said,
No; for we will flee upon horses; therefore shall ye
flee: and, We will ride upon the swift; therefore shall
they that pursue you be swift" (Isa. 30:15-16).

The Lord waits that He might be gracious

The Lord was actually waiting to see who would be found *waiting*. The Lord wanted to be very gracious unto them! This trial was doing something within the inhabitants of Zion. They were just crying out to the Lord (rending their hearts, as it says in the book of Joel, 2:12-14). The remnant that remained and trusted and cried out to the Lord saw the mighty deliverance upon Mount Zion. They saw the Northern army removed.

The Lord comes through

We all know the end of the story—God saved Zion with a mighty victory. However, let us now consider a few of the things that this siege accomplished:

- They saw the power of the enemy broken. 185,000 Assyrians died on the hills around the city, and they never fired an arrow. (See Isa. 37:33, and 2 Kgs. 19:35.)
- The fame of that victory went to the nations, and the nations sent gifts and honors to Zion. (See 2 Chr. 32:22, and Psa. 76.)
- The remnant that had submitted to the siege was called "holy" (Isa. 4:3).

- The Assyrians, who had plundered the nations, left "mountains of spoil' for the victors (Isa. 33:23, Psa. 76:4). Psalm 76 is a Psalm of their victory over Sennacherib.
- Those who had remained in the city were given a promise of having the Lord's gracious favor: "He shall dwell on high: his place of defense shall be the munitions of rocks: bread shall be given him; his waters shall be sure" (Isa. 33:16).
- "Thine eyes shall see the king in his beauty: they shall behold the land that is very far off" (Isa. 33:17).
- The lame and the feeble remnant was healed of all their diseases: "And the inhabitant shall not say, I am sick: the people that dwell therein shall be forgiven their iniquity" (Isa. 33:24).

The anointing breaks the yoke

Isaiah 10:12 - "Wherefore it shall come to pass, that when the Lord hath performed his whole work upon mount Zion and on Jerusalem, I will punish the fruit of the stout heart of the king of Assyria, and the glory of his high looks." Do you see why the enemy is still allowed to exist even today? God uses the

enemy to perfect His people, and when they are no
longer needed in our life, the anointing breaks their
yoke of bondage! Often, Christians are more
concerned with destroying the enemy than trying to
discover why the enemy is there. "And the yoke
shall be destroyed because of the anointing"
(Isa.10:27).

The captivity and the restoration of Zion

We are now jumping to another event that would
take place about 100 years later. The captivity of
Zion began in approximately 606 BC until the
release in 536 BC. This is known as the Babylonian
Captivity, which lasted seventy years. This is a
completely different scenario of Zion's redemption.
The siege during the time of Hezekiah was a trial in
which the Lord said to *stay* in the city and trust Him
for His redemption. On the other hand, *the captivity*
was a trial in which the Lord said to *surrender* to the
enemy, and in doing so, this would be their redemption. (See Jeremiah chapter 27.)

The remnant

Although there are other truths disclosed
through the captivity, basically the same results were
going to be accomplished through both of these

trials. The Lord was going to find a remnant of people who would be perfected through this tribulation and come forth from the others! Among His people, God has always had a remnant who have experienced the *fullness* of salvation! (Heb. 7:25).

As in the trial of Job, God subjected some very good men to a captivity through which He would cleanse them from something and ultimately make them even greater. All of those who have a message of restoration have first experienced a "captivity!"

Zion/Jerusalem was very backslidden at the time of the captivity; yet there was a remnant who, along with Jeremiah, were mourning for the sins of the land: "And the LORD said unto him, Go through the midst of the city, through the midst of Jerusalem, and set a mark upon the foreheads of the men that sigh and that cry for all the abominations that be done in the midst thereof" (Ezek. 9:4). Those who were sealed by the angel in this vision were marked for redemption and preservation.

The vision of the basket of figs

Jeremiah's vision of the two baskets of figs capsules the message very well. The good basket of figs would go into captivity. (The figs obviously represent people.) There in the captivity God would "give them a heart to know Him." The captives would ultimately return with their whole heart.

"Thus saith the LORD, the God of Israel; Like these good figs, so will I acknowledge them that are carried away captive of Judah, whom I have sent out of this place into the land of the Chaldeans for their good. For I will set mine eyes upon them for good, and I will bring them again to this land: and I will build them, and not pull them down; and I will plant them, and not pluck them up. And I will give them an heart to know me, that I am the LORD: and they shall be my people, and I will be their God: for they shall return unto me with their whole heart" (Jer. 24:5-7).

Part of the redemptive process

"Captivities" do not necessarily come because people are wicked. It is a part of the divine process of regeneration. Matthew 1:17 states: "So all the generations from Abraham to David are fourteen generations; and from David until the carrying away into Babylon are fourteen generations; and from the carrying away into Babylon unto Christ are fourteen generations." Notice that there are three equal stages of Israel's development:

- Abraham to David   Time of wandering.
- David to Babylon   Time of cleansing.

- Babylon to Christ   The real work is done.
                           (Restored to the image
                           of Christ.)

Perhaps we could summarize Jeremiah's message in one verse. In Jeremiah 1:10, God said to the prophet: "See, I have this day set thee over the nations and over the kingdoms, to root out, and to pull down, and to destroy, and to throw down, to build, and to plant". Before Jeremiah could build and plant, there were many things that first had to be rooted up and destroyed. We become the *"true message"* after there has been much uprooting in our lives. The old Adam and the new Adam cannot coexist; the old man must die. Babylon was necessary to cleanse God's people from their pride and their idols. Babylon worked a *revulsion* of idolatry, as the people were forced to worship idols.

A personal experience

For a moment I would like to relate a personal experience that bears out this message. Years ago I found myself in one situation after another, and these situations were strikingly similar—the same kind of atmosphere, the same kind of music, and even the same kind of people seemed to dominate the scene. I asked the Lord why I was continually subjected to these seemingly inescapable conditions. The Lord began to impress upon me a certain portion of Scripture from 2 Kings chapter 5 concerning Naaman the leper. As you will remember, the Lord did not cleanse this man in the pure waters of Damascus as he requested, but it was in the filthy waters of Jordan that he was cleansed, after seven repeat sessions. I began to understand that the Lord was cleansing me through the very atmosphere that I had come to despise.

To those who refuse

Jeremiah also tells us the outcome of those who *refuse* captivity; he uses Moab to illustrate this truth. Moab had refused captivity from his youth. He is likened to wine that is sitting stagnant in a vessel that has never been poured. In the bottom of this vessel was bitter sediment which tainted the wine.

"Moab hath been at ease from his youth, and he hath settled on his lees [or dregs], and hath not been emptied from vessel to vessel, neither hath he gone into captivity: therefore his taste remained in him, and his scent is not changed" (Jer. 48:11). Those who refuse the captivity of the Lord retain the "old scent" of the Adamic nature, and thus, they are undesirable. Actually, those who rebelled against the Babylonian captivity were destroyed.

When the Lord shall build up Zion, He shall appear in His glory

Babylon was the place that would cleanse those who would possess the true message of restoration. The restoration movement of the Ezra / Nehemiah period was only *a figure* of the restoration of the Church of Zion. When the truths of Mount Zion have been restored indeed, the Lord shall appear in His glory! (See Psa.102:16.)

After the temple and the city were finally rebuilt (444 B. C.), there was a great revival at the water gate. This event took place during the Feast of Tabernacles. (See Neh. Ch. 8.) The revival was then followed by a jubilant rededication of the city (Neh.12:27-43). Those who had invested their lives with sweat and tears were now rejoicing upon the walls: "... So that the joy of Jerusalem was heard even afar off" (Neh.12:43).

Revival psalms of the Restoration Era

The last five Psalms (Psalms 146-150) reflect this era of history. We will find a number of the miracles of Christ in these Psalms. There is exuberant praise in the midst of God's people. All of these five Psalms are called *"Hallelujah Psalms."*

Psalm 146:7-8 - "Which executeth judgment for

the oppressed: which giveth food to the hungry. The LORD looseth the prisoners: The LORD openeth the eyes of the blind: the LORD raiseth them that are bowed down: the LORD loveth the righteous."

Psalm 147:2-3 - The backsliders are restored: "The LORD doth build up Jerusalem: he gathereth together the outcasts of Israel. He healeth the broken in heart, and bindeth up their wounds."

Psalm 149:6-9 - Judgment has again been given to the saints: "Let the high praises of God be in their mouth, and a twoedged sword in their hand; To execute vengeance upon the heathen, and punishments upon the people; To bind their kings with chains, and their nobles with fetters of iron; To execute upon them the judgment written: this honour have all his saints. Praise ye the LORD."

Psalm 150:6 - These Psalms end with the grand finale of the Church. As a grand symphony, all are in unity, all are in time and in tune with their Heavenly conductor: "Let every thing that hath breath praise the LORD. Praise ye the LORD."

CHAPTER FIFTEEN

The End of David — The End of The Church

In this chapter, we are going to draw an analogy from David's final days to bring out some important points concerning the last-day Church. At the end of David's reign, there seems to be a clean sweep of many that had retained their positions, and yet were not worthy of them. We shall see the unrighteous removed and the righteous exalted. "Then shall the righteous shine forth as the sun in the kingdom of their Father. Who hath ears to hear, let him hear" (Mt.13:43).

David's life a figure to the Church

As we have learned in this study, David is a type of the Church Age. Also, he is a type of the high calling to those within the Church.

- His calling to reign
- His wilderness dealings
- His three anointings
- His apprehension of Zion
- His function in the Melchizedek order
- His dominion over the nations
- His great blessing
- His bringing forth of the Christ (It was through his own loins that the Christ came.)

What David had experienced upon Mount Zion was the true order of the Church. That order must be restored, according to Amos: "In that day will I raise up the tabernacle of David that is fallen, and close up the breaches thereof; and I will raise up his ruins, and I will build it as in the days of old" (Amos 9:11). This is reconfirmed by James in Acts 15:16-17.

The Church has not yet fulfilled this

Especially notice how Amos 9:11 ends: "I will build it again *as in the days of old.*" I don't think that we can say that the Church at any time in its history (AD 30 to 2000) has ever fully been restored to the pattern of David's Tabernacle – certainly not the Church at large. The nations have not sought its covering, and in no wise is the Church at this time complete. Therefore, it must be the Church of the last days that shall have the greatest realization of this restoration. The Church of this generation seems to be just awakening to the trumpet call.

Is it over for David?

David had a very great fall; it was as though the latter part of his life was consumed with judgments. When you take a look at the end of David's life, you see him as old and feeble and unable to arise. "Now King David was old and stricken in years; and they covered him with clothes, but he gat no heat" (1 Kings 1:1). In this account we see David pictured as an old, decrepit king that has seemingly lost the anointing. As the scene progresses, his attendants try to revive David through some very fleshly means. It is like a revival or a move of God that is over, and yet there are those who seek to revive something that has served its purpose. (See 1 Kings chapter 1.)

As the title of this chapter suggests, the end of the Church Age seems to fit here. It looks like the Church is about to die and has had its day of glory.

Today many are trying to revive the Church through their illicit means: trying to bring in the young people with music that appeals to the flesh, trying to salvage families through psychology programs, and compromising standards to save *"poor David."*

Actually, the Lord has good plans for David, who really is not as poor as some might think. This little interim at the end of the age proves to be very necessary to clear away those who are not loyal to David. When the dissenters are gone, the fullness of blessing comes upon the righteous.

Adonijah (1 Kings 1:5 - 2:25)

1 Kings 1:5 - "Then Adonijah the son of Haggith exalted himself, saying, I will be king: and he prepared him chariots and horsemen, and fifty men to run before him." Adonijah was the key instrument that God would use to clear away those within the kingdom that were not real loyal. Adonijah was a son of David; he was gifted and he had leadership ability. But like many gifted people, he was *assuming* to take a position that God had clearly designated for another.

We should never be confused on this point. Giftings alone do not qualify anyone for a leadership position. Giftings without character equals pride, and pride is very deceptive. In fact, Satan's pride deceived him: "The pride of thine heart hath deceived thee" (Obadiah 1:3). Satan had ambition. See the five "I will's" of Satan in Isaiah 14:13-14.

Adonijah - a type of the Anti-Christ

In many ways Adonijah can be seen as a type of the anti-christ. He wanted the throne of David, even as Satan wants the throne of the greater son of David. Adonijah's character is revealed in those from whom he solicited support. He only solicited support from *fellow offenders*. He never conferred with those who were upright. "And he conferred with Joab the son of Zeruiah, and with Abiathar the priest: and they following Adonijah helped him. But Zadok the priest, and Benaiah the son of Jehoiada, and Nathan the prophet, and Shimei, and Rei, and the mighty men which belonged to David, were not with Adonijah" (1 Kgs.1:7).

Adonijah's actions, in effect, are a fulfillment of the parable of the tares and the wheat: "The Son of man shall send forth his angels, and they shall gather out of his kingdom all things that offend, and them which do iniquity … Then shall the righteous shine forth as the sun in the kingdom of their Father. Who hath ears to hear, let him hear" (Mt.13:36-43). The word "angels" in the above passage can be translated *messengers* or *ministers*. After the offenders had been gathered together for Adonijah's coronation banquet, then David arose and inaugurated the real government. (See 1 Kings 1:32-52.) The offenders were scattered like chaff in the wind.

David revives

"So when David was old and full of days, he made Solomon his son king over Israel. And he gathered together all the princes of Israel, with the priests and the Levites" (1 Chr. 23:1). Also, judging from 1 Chronicles 23-26, 28-29, David appointed the 24 courses of priests, musicians, and porters *after* Solomon's inauguration. This means that David had quite a reviving. They also had a second coronation service for Solomon because the first one was not that auspicious.

It was during this revival of David, that Solomon was given the charge to build the Temple. David also gave to Solomon the pattern of the temple which he had received from the Lord, and he committed all of the great provision that had been stored up into Solomon's hand.

David came out of his molt with great power to bless Israel and to magnify the Lord. Yet, what is so interesting about this whole scene was the transition that took place right at the end of David's life. It is as though there was a changing of the guard right at the end of the Mount Zion era. All of the chronic offenders were removed, and there was a clean sweep of the leadership. See below:

- Adonijah, the self-exalted leader is removed.
- Joab, the elder who cannot be corrected is removed.
- Abiathar, the compromising priest from Eli's line is removed.
- All the other offenders such as Shimei are dealt with.

All of these men had serious character flaws that were *never* corrected in life.

"Then shall the righteous shine forth"

The new administration was put into place before David passed from the scene. This is the government that shall usher in the Millennium or the new age. In a figure, Solomon speaks of the Millennial age, even as David represents the Church Age.

- *Solomon* assumed his rightful throne. *Adonijah* was put to death.
- *Benaiah* replaced Joab as the captain of the host. *Joab* was put to death.

- *Zadok* replaced Abiathar as the high priest.
  Abiathar was thrust out of office.

All these men who had prominent positions and yet had never corrected their offences were finally swept out at the end of David's life. They were like the "hypocrites in Zion" mentioned in Isaiah 33:14. The Church Age will end with the righteous being in authority. The Eli line of priests will give way to the righteous Zadok priesthood, and all of the righteous shall triumph in the end.

David's end is glorious

1 Chronicles 29:28 - "And he died in a good old age, full of days, riches, and honour." The end of David was very glorious and the end of this Church Age will also be glorious. Of course, these truths of David are just figures of the real. At the end of this age, "David" will not die, but receive immortality to reign with Christ—those who are found worthy.

> *"And it shall come to pass in the last days..."*
>
> *(Isaiah 2:2)*

Isaiah 2:2-3 - "And it shall come to pass in the

last days, that the mountain of the Lord's house shall be established in the top of the mountains, and shall be exalted above the hills; and all nations shall flow unto it. And many people shall go and say, Come ye, and let us go up to the mountain of the LORD, to the house of the God of Jacob; and he will teach us of his ways, and we will walk in his paths: for out of Zion shall go forth the law, and the word of the LORD from Jerusalem."

As we have previously explained, these truths have literal relevance to Israel in the Millennium. However, the Church must first experience them spiritually. This government that has been set into place upon spiritual Zion shall now teach the nations the laws of God. The *"Zadok priesthood"* shall now declare things the way that they are.

It is as though the nations are now hungry to know His ways. I believe the time is coming when the nations of the earth will realize that they do not have the answers! This indeed would be the fulfillment of Acts 15:15-17. The true order of David's Tabernacle has been restored, and now the nations (Gentiles) are seeking unto its covering. "I will return, and will build again the tabernacle of David, which is fallen down... That the residue of men might seek after the Lord, and all the Gentiles, upon whom my name is called."

Again, we should notice the distinction between

Jerusalem and Zion. According to Isaiah 2:3, the *law* goes forth from Zion, and the word of the Lord from Jerusalem. The *law* of the Lord is what is missing from the Church today—the law written within the hearts. Consider these three levels:

Zion	The Holy of Holies (The law was in the holy of holies.)
Jerusalem	The Holy Place
Judah	The Outer Court

Psalm 76:2
"In Salem also is his tabernacle, and his dwelling place in Zion."

The assemblies upon Mount Zion

Isaiah 4:5-6 - "And the LORD will create upon every dwelling place of mount Zion, and upon her assemblies, a cloud and smoke by day, and the shining of a flaming fire by night: for upon all the glory shall be a defense."

Here is a verse that has its greatest relevance for the Church. In fact, we would have a difficult time trying to place this verse into any of Israel's past history. It would have to relate to the final siege of Jerusalem, when the Lord comes and saves Zion (Zech.14:2-3). Half of the city remains when the

Lord returns. It is the Mount Zion half that remains.

"For I will gather all nations against Jerusalem to battle; and the city shall be taken, and the houses rifled, and the women ravished; and half of the city shall go forth into captivity, and the residue of the people shall not be cut off from the city. Then shall the LORD go forth, and fight against those nations, as when he fought in the day of battle. And his feet shall stand in that day upon the Mount of Olives" (Zec.14:2-4).

Without question, it is the Church of the last days (those congregations that have been brought to the spiritual Zion) which shall manifest His glory. As the glory of the Lord protected Israel when they came out of Egypt, so shall His glory be the defense of the Church! (See Ex.14:19-20.) The passage in Isaiah continues: "And there shall be a tabernacle for a shadow in the daytime from the heat, and for a place of refuge, and for a covert from storm and from rain" (Isaiah 4:6).

Zion is not an organization that we can join. It is a dimension in God that only the consecrated can know. As the Psalmist said: "He that dwelleth in the secret place of the most High shall abide under the shadow of the Almighty" (Psa. 91:1).

In the 1950's, there was a church in our city that was experiencing quite a revival. On several occasions, the local fire department was called there to put out the fire. There was no fire, but what people were seeing was a manifestation of God's glory that gave the appearance of the building's being on fire.

Last day covering of Zion

In the last days of this age, revival and judgments are intermingled. A good picture of this would be the ten plagues of Egypt. God's prophet was releasing plague after plague upon Egypt, yet Israel was *sheltered* right in the midst of the tribulation: "And Moses stretched forth his hand toward heaven; and there was a thick darkness in all the land of Egypt three days: They saw not one another, neither rose any from his place for three days: but all the children of Israel had light in their dwellings" (Ex.10:22-23).

Many who are not abiding in this secret place (cf. Psalm 91) will undergo the same judgments as the world. It is interesting that the mercy seat is represented by the covering wings of the cherubims upon the Ark (Ex. 25:20). Of course, the Ark is upon Mount Zion. The last-day Church is a fully redeemed Church. It is a Church that has been glorified. May we as leaders seek to bring our assemblies up to His dwelling place into the full New Covenant reality of Mount Zion. At this point, let us pause and have a slight review of our study on David's Tabernacle:

Review

- David's Tabernacle is often synonymous with Mount Zion by virtue of the fact that David planted it thereupon.
- David's Tabernacle (Mount Zion) represents the place of the Lord's abiding love: "The LORD loveth the gates of Zion more than all the dwellings of Jacob" (Psa. 87:2).
- David's Tabernacle pictures the unveiled Ark of the Covenant, and therefore speaks of the manifest presence of God.
- David's Tabernacle not only represents the rent veil, but the people who have entered in. Theoretically, we are seated with Christ in heavenly places, but then there has to be the reality of this. Ascending the holy hill must become one's *experience.*
- David's Tabernacle foreshadows what the Church (in its highest dimension) is intended to portray.
- David's Tabernacle represents the New Covenant reality. The New Covenant is the fulfillment of Jeremiah 31:31-34 and Ezekiel 36:26-27. It is the law written upon the heart. The tables of stone, were in this tent contained in the unveiled Ark.
- David's Tabernacle (Mount Zion) represents

the "perfection of beauty" (Psa. 50:2). It also represents those who have become complete or perfect. (See Mt. 5:48.) God's purpose is the highest plane and anything less is falling short of the mark (Rom.3:23). To be a 30-fold or a 60-fold Christian is to fall short of God's 100-fold maxim. Perfection is relative. It is reckoned to us as we maintain a proper rate of growth. For example, a child can be perfect at his growth level as long as he is continuing to grow.

- David's Tabernacle represents a people that have qualified. They have fulfilled Psalm fifteen, and Psalm twenty-four. They have had the song of the pilgrim worked out in their hearts. (See Chapter 11.) They are a people in unity.

- David's Tabernacle (Mount Zion) represents those who inherit the birthright blessing, or the blessing of the firstborn. (See Chapter 13.)

- David's Tabernacle gives us a beautiful picture of the Melchizedek Order to which we are called. (See 1 Pet. 2:5, 9.)

- David's Tabernacle represents the higher dimension of worship and praise. David introduced a new ministry of worship and praise before the Ark. Not only does anointed music bring the presence of God, the Lord *inhabits* the praises of His people (Psa. 22:3).

- David's Tabernacle represents the calling to all nations to be kings, and priests. "And hast redeemed us to God by thy blood out of every kindred, and tongue, and people, and nation; And hast made us unto our God kings and priests: and we shall reign on the earth" (Rev. 5:9-10; cf. Acts 15:16-17).

- David's Tabernacle (Mount Zion) represents those who shall inherit the nations and those who will rule the nations with Christ. (See Psa. 2:8, Rev.12:5.) The new government was formed under the Mount Zion order.

- David's Tabernacle represents Christ seated in his Church and ruling through His Church in righteous judgments (Isa.16:5).

- David's Tabernacle (Mount Zion) represents the higher standard because the law goes forth from Zion (See Mic. 4:2). Also, the *Stone* that is laid in Zion is Christ, and every doctrine must measure to this stone. (See Isa. 28:16-17, and 1 Pet. 2:6.)

- David's Tabernacle (Mount Zion) represents the place that God defends or that God fights for. Isaiah tells us that *"His glory"* shall be the defense of it! (See Isa. 4:5-6.)

- David's Tabernacle speaks of the people that shall bear His presence and glory and authority to the Church of the last days. As those who had been ordained upon Mount Zion brought the Ark down to his Temple, so shall it be in the last day Church.

- David's Tabernacle (Mount Zion) represents those who shall teach the nations "His ways" (Isa. 2:2-3). Zion of the last days represents a great catch of fish (Isa. 60:1-5).

- The truths and reality of David's Tabernacle shall fully be restored to the Church. (See Amos 9:11, and Acts 15:16-17). Zion of the last days shall be redeemed!

CHAPTER SIXTEEN

New Testament Exhortation to Zion

In this final chapter we will consider one of the most dominant (if not the *most* dominant) themes in the book of Hebrews, which is—"Let us go on..." The Church in Jerusalem should have been one of the most advanced of all the Christian churches. Yet it was reverting back to the Old Covenant, even returning to physical sacrifices.

The author continually shows them the inferiority of the Old Covenant and urges them to enter into the fullness of the *better* covenant that was wrought for them in Christ. Paul uses the word *"better"* thirteen times in this epistle. His contrast of the two mountains, Sinai and Zion, best integrates the theme of this epistle to the Hebrews. "Ye are not come to Mount Sinai...but ye are come to Mount Zion" (Heb.12:18,22). The author turns the focus to Mount Zion because it is here that the New Covenant is symbolized.

The Church was not moving

As we examine the message of Hebrews in light of what we have already studied, we can see that the Apostle is trying to awaken the Church to move on to the higher call. Jerusalem was in a stupor; they were even losing their grip on the elementary doctrines. Paul said in one place, "Ye have need that one come and teach you again" (5:12). It is interesting that all of the *"big name"* ministry were in Jerusalem. They had the best teachers in the world. Their teachers had been taught by the Master Himself, and undoubtedly this Church was the best-versed Church in the empire.

The Church was dull of hearing

I don't think the problem was that they were not being taught, but rather it was in their insensitivity to hear what God was saying. Paul told them, "Ye are dull of hearing" (Heb. 5:11).

Hebrews 2:1

"Therefore we ought to give the more earnest heed to the things which we have heard, lest at any time we should let them slip." They were not paying attention.

Hebrews 4:7

"Again, he limiteth a certain day, saying in David, To day, after so long a time; as it is said, To day if ye will hear his voice, harden not your hearts." *If you will hear his voice—* There is something about over-familiarity with truth that causes insensitivity. Hearing the same message over and over with no response is very dangerous. It is like hearing an alarm clock that we comfortably sleep through by continually hitting the snooze button. (See Amos 8:11).

They had paid a price

It is so easy to camp on lower levels and to stop short of God's best. This Church had been through a tremendous conflict. In fact, Paul reminds them of this: "But call to remembrance the former days, in which, after ye were illuminated, ye endured a great fight of afflictions; Partly, whilst ye were made a gazingstock both by reproaches and afflictions; and partly, whilst ye became companions of them that were so used. For ye had compassion of me in my bonds, and took joyfully the spoiling of your goods, knowing in yourselves that ye have in heaven a better and an enduring substance" (Heb.10:32-34).

The saints in Jerusalem had been through a long trial of their faith but now were willing to coexist and find acceptance among their former persecutors. This is why the Apostle is urging the saints not to camp, not to compromise, not to modify the doctrine of Christ, but to endure the reproach of Christ by going on. "Let us go forth therefore unto him without the camp, bearing his reproach" (Heb.13:13).

There is something about *going on* that brings great resistance from the enemy. Life can become much easier when we *camp* and opt to stay on the present plane. In fact, there can even be a certain blessing achieved because we have attained to a certain plateau. We can enter an inheritance, even if it is not the full reward. Two-and-a-half tribes proved this when they stopped short of crossing the Jordan and entered into an inheritance early. This helps us to understand what Paul is saying in chapters three and four as he exhorts them to labor to enter into the rest and not to fall short because of unbelief.

Zion, the "rest" of God

Psalm 132:13-14 - "For the LORD hath chosen Zion; he hath desired it for his habitation. This is my rest forever: here will I dwell; for I have desired it." Zion is a picture of *the rest* that God's people are exhorted to enter into. How do we describe such a dimension in God where suddenly our strength ceases and the divine takes over? We will consider a few examples in this chapter, but for the moment let us consider Samson. Here is a man who rips the city gates off the wall (perhaps weighing several tons), and then he carries them twenty miles, and up a hill. Was he sweating? I don't think so, at least not until the anointing lifted. Samson had entered into a dimension where the supernatural was doing the work. (See Jud.16:3.)

Chapters three and four of Hebrews mentions *"the rest"* eleven times:

- Hebrews 3:11
"So I sware in my wrath, They shall not enter into my *rest.*"

- Hebrews 3:18
"And to whom sware he that they should not enter into his *rest,* but to them that believed not?"

- Hebrews 4:1

"Let us therefore fear, lest, a promise being left us of entering into his *rest,* any of you should seem to come short of it."

- Hebrews 4:3

"For we which have believed do enter into *rest,* as he said, As I have sworn in my wrath, if they shall enter into my *rest:* although the works were finished from the foundation of the world."

- Hebrews 4:4

"For he spake in a certain place of the seventh day on this wise, And God did *rest* the seventh day from all his works."

- Hebrews 4:5

"And in this place again, If they shall enter into my *rest.*"

- Hebrews 4:8

"If Jesus had given them *rest,* then would he not afterward have spoken of another day."

- Hebrews 4:9-10

"There remaineth therefore *a rest* to the

people of God. For he that is entered into his *rest,* he also hath ceased from his own works, as God did from his."

• Hebrews 4:11
"Let us labour therefore to enter into that *rest,* lest any man fall after the same example of unbelief."

There are many analogies of this *"rest"* found in Scripture, such as marriage, but essentially "the rest" is associated with the Ark of the Covenant. Israel was commanded to follow the Ark, and this Ark would ultimately bring them into His rest: "And they departed from the mount of the LORD three days' journey: and the Ark of the covenant of the LORD went before them in the three days' journey, to search out a resting place for them" (Num.10:33). God was eventually bringing His people to His holy mountain (Mount Zion), into the holy of holies.

Mount Zion is the high calling to the Church Age, the call to come within the veil. David's Tabernacle housed the Ark, and there was no veil in this tabernacle. This is the ultimate rest and the invitation is to all. Christ rent the veil for us, showing us the way in. However, as the author of Hebrews warns: "Let us therefore fear, lest, a promise being left us of entering into his rest, any of you should seem to come short of it" (Heb. 4:1). This charge is to the New Testament saints!

The land of promise

Let's examine a few of the examples that Paul gives concerning those who failed to enter, and why. Paul is using Old Testament analogies here. "For unto us was the gospel preached, as well as unto them: but the word preached did not profit them, not being mixed with faith in them that heard it" (Heb. 4:2). Paul uses Israel's failure to enter the land of promise as a figure that might provoke a *"godly fear."* Israel had heard the message of this place of *rest* that God desired to bring them into, but they did not believe! "But with whom was he grieved forty years? was it not with them that had sinned, whose carcasses fell in the wilderness? And to whom sware he that they should not enter into his rest, but to them that believed not? So we see that they could not enter in because of unbelief" (Heb. 3:17-19).

Joshua did not bring them in

Paul warns the New Testament saints not to fail after the same manner of unbelief. The Apostle says: "We have heard the message as well as they. What shall we do with this message of the higher plane? Do we believe that we have such a hope? Shall we claim unworthiness? Shall we continue to be content with our present experience? Shall we harden our hearts to this delightsome land, to this fruitful land flowing with spiritual and natural blessing?" The writer of Hebrews knew that all of these Old Testament examples were only figures of the real land of promise. Note Hebrews 4:8 - "For if Jesus [Joshua] had given them rest, then would he not afterward have spoken of another day." In this passage, *Jesus* is the Greek rendition of "Joshua."

Joshua was a type of Christ as our Captain, the One who brings us into the inheritance reserved for the saints. However, as you can see from the above verse, Joshua only brought them into rest in a figure: "Remember the word which Moses the servant of the LORD commanded you, saying, The LORD your God hath given you rest, and hath given you this land ... Until the LORD have given your brethren rest, as he hath given you, and they also have possessed the land which the LORD your God giveth them: then ye shall return unto the land of your possession, and enjoy it" (Josh.1:13,15). Yet, there is another day spoken of, and there *yet remains a rest* to the people of God.

The Seventh Day

Paul also uses the Sabbath to symbolize what this rest is all about: "For he spake in a certain place of the seventh day on this wise, And God did rest the seventh day from all his works ... For he that is entered into his rest, he also hath ceased from his own works, as God did from his" (Heb 4:4,10). The Sabbath day is symbolic of ceasing from the works of the flesh. "Six days shalt thou labour." Six is the number of man. Man had to cease from his physical labor on the seventh day.

The seventh day is also a figure of the Millennium. (See Isaiah chapter 11:10.) "His rest shall be glorious." The Millennium is a thousand year reign of peace and tranquility. "The whole earth is at rest, and is quiet: they break forth into singing" (Isa.14:7). One reason the earth is at rest is because Satan and his cohorts have been removed, but I want us to concentrate on this thought of "ceasing from the works of the flesh."

Jesus also explained the Sabbath in John 5:9-19. In this narrative Jesus is accused of healing a man on the Sabbath. Jesus responds to this by saying: "My Father *worketh* hitherto, and I *work*." Jesus was in the true rest of His Father. He was not performing anything at his own whim or desire; He was not moving in His own strength, but in perfect accord with heaven.

John 5:19 - "Then answered Jesus and said unto them, Verily, verily, I say unto you, The Son can do nothing of himself, but what he seeth the Father do: for what things soever he doeth, these also doeth the Son likewise." This is what the true rest is all about. It is a cessation of our works, our thoughts, our ambitions, our human cleverness, and it is God doing the work through us.

Laboring to enter into rest

"And he saw them toiling in rowing; for the wind was contrary unto them" (Mk. 6:48). In this narrative, Jesus had commissioned his disciples to go to the other side of Lake Galilee, and they were putting forth a lot of physical effort to accomplish this. Much of our Christian experience is like this, as we are working hard to bring to pass things that Jesus has commissioned us to do. We might be working in a very legitimate manner, but sometimes we even get into the flesh trying to accomplish God's work. When we get into the flesh we can produce an "Ishmael."

Then Jesus comes on the scene and He enters the boat. This was the result: "Then they willingly received him into the ship: and immediately the ship was at the land whither they went" (Jn. 6:21). Immediately they arrived at their destination. I think this helps us to understand the exhortation to *"labor to enter into rest."* The disciples were commanded to go to the other side and they were working to get there, but when Jesus appeared they immediately arrived!

Today if you will hear His Voice

"Again, he limiteth a certain day, saying in David, To day, after so long a time; as it is said, To day if ye will hear his voice, harden not your hearts" (Heb. 4:7). Paul is addressing this to the New Testament saints, hoping that they will not fail after the same manner of unbelief as some of their predecessors. The word *"today"* means TODAY. It means that this message is just as relevant in this 20-21st century as it was in David's time when the invitation to ascend Zion's hill was declared.

David had entered that rest; He had experienced God's subduing the enemy through his hand. "And it came to pass, when the king sat in his house, and the LORD had given him *rest* round about from all his enemies..." (2 Sam. 7:1). David had experienced (in a figure) the reality of entering the rent veil and seeing the Lord make all of his enemies his footstool. However, David was concerned for his own generation when he said: "TODAY, if you will hear his voice…" (Psa. 95:7). "God limits a day" in every generation. For those who continually hear and do not respond, the invitation discontinues.

Let us fear

Hebrews 4:1,6 - "Let us therefore fear, lest, a promise being left us of entering into his rest, any of you should seem to come short of it … Seeing therefore it remaineth that some must enter therein, and they to whom it was first preached entered not in because of unbelief." I think the message is quite clear. In every generation some will hear and appropriate that call, and some will not. Let us take heed to ourselves that we fail not: "There remaineth therefore a rest to the people of God" (Heb. 4:9).

But ye are come to Mount Zion
(Hebrews 12:22)

Hebrews 12:18, 22 - "For ye are not come unto the mount that might be touched, and that burned with fire, nor unto blackness, and darkness, and tempest … But ye are come unto mount Sion ." The mount that might be touched was the physical Mount Sinai where they received the "Old Covenant." The mount Zion that we are come to cannot be touched because it speaks of the spiritual or heavenly dimension. In the context in which these two mountains are in contrast, we are considering the Old Covenant versus the New Covenant.

As we have already learned, Mount Zion represents the New Covenant because the Ark was sitting there in David's unveiled tabernacle. The New Covenant is apprehendable for all who believe and put their belief into action. If we say that we believe something and then walk contrary to that belief, we will not have it. Many of the Hebrews were reverting to their traditions and to a religion that had no power to perfect them.

The Apostle Paul had earlier in the book of Hebrews made a very important statement that we now want to consider: "For we which have believed do enter into rest, as he said, As I have sworn in my wrath, *if they shall enter into* my rest: although the works were finished from the foundation of the world" (Heb. 4:3).

Many people have the notion that because God has accomplished something for us, we automatically possess it. Salvation was accomplished for us before the foundation of the world. Salvation was procured for all men, yet not all men will be saved. Healing was also made available to us 2000 years ago, yet not everyone believes in healing or receives it.

The question posed to us in this verse is: *"...if they shall enter in."* The same question remains concerning this high calling of God to the Church. Although the way has been opened, although there is grace to attain to this abiding place, WILL WE ENTER IN?

Epilogue

*"And I looked, and lo, [the] Lamb stood
on the mount Sion"*

(Revelation 14:1)

In one sense, Christ Himself is the Tabernacle
of David, and therefore, to enter in is to enter the
fullness of Christ!

As we conclude this study of David's Tabernacle,
again I would like us to visualize Mount Zion, not
with the Ark resting there, but with the One whom the
Ark symbolized standing there—"the Lamb of God."
Not only is the Lamb standing on Mount Zion, there
is also a special group of people who are standing
with Him on this mount – those who have overcome
(Rev. 14:1-5). These have hit the mark, won the prize,

and attained unto the high calling of God in Christ Jesus. Those who *win Christ* have won all things (Phil. 3:10-14). But for a brief moment, let us go back to the upper room upon Mount Zion and see the Lamb washing the feet of His disciples. Here you will recall what Jesus said: "If I wash thee not, thou hast no part with me" (Jn.13:8).

As you know, the disciples had quite an upset that night. Those eleven disciples were shaken traumatically, and they were scattered. Yet, fifty-four days later they were in that same upper room again upon Mount Zion, being endowed with power from on high. From the unction that was received from heaven on the Day of Pentecost, they brought the glory down to fill the Temple of "His Body"—the Church.

The pattern seems so clear; those who ascend Mount Zion find themselves on trial, being washed, being dealt with, and being measured by the "Cornerstone of Zion." But then Zion's mourning is over, and the inhabitants of Zion possess the double portion of His Spirit to perform the greater works of Christ. So be it, Lord! (See Isaiah 61:3-7).

> *"What shall one then answer the messengers of the nation? That the LORD hath founded Zion, and the poor of his people shall trust in it"*
>
> *(Isaiah 14:32).*

Printed in the United States
28192LVS00005B/30